gourmet food with all of the flavor and none of the guilt

THE GUILT FREE GOURMET

Low Point & Calorie Cooking Guide - 2020
COOKBOOK VOLUME 1

Follow me online at:

The Web: www.theguiltfreegourmet.net
Connect: @dhallakx7
Facebook: The Guilt Free Gourmet LLC.
Instagram: TheGuiltFreeGourmet ... No, seriously... Follow me on Instagram.
Youtube Channel: The Guilt Free Gourmet ... I'll be uploading a lot of fun cooking vids soon! Subscribe please!
You can find this book, as well as my Cookbook, on Amazon.com
(not to be confused with that old vegan, gluten free, hippie dessert book of the same name... That's not mine)

LEGAL DISCLAIMERS:

The Guilt Free Gourmet ® 2019

Though we have copyright protection over this publication and the materials here-in,
we at The Guilt Free Gourmet want to make sure you understand that **you have
our full and complete permission to have this material printed for your private use**!
**If you are a home cook or a cooking enthusiast, please know that we wish for you to be able
to print this material, either at home, or at a business that offers printing services, such as
Staples, Office Depot, Kinkos, etc.**

If you try to take this to a printing center and they say that they can't print it,
PLEASE tell them to look at the disclaimer cited above. The Author has expressly
stated that he (me) has given permission for you to print it... Then poke him/her in the
chest to establish dominance. Howling loudly while pointing at their copy machine.

Weight Watchers International & WW ®

The Guilt Free Gourmet is not affiliated with, nor is it endorsed by
Weight Watchers International, Inc. (now WW®). Weight Watchers has not reviewed
this publication for accuracy or suitability for WW members.

Weight Watchers, WW®, Point, Points, Smart Points, SP's and Freestyle, are all registered
trademarks of Weight Watchers International, Inc. Authentic information about
the program is only available at your local WW workshop or online through the
WW website and mobile app. The information and recipes contained within this guide
are based solely on the recollections and assumptions of The Guilt Free Gourmet.
The information and recipes are not warranted for any purpose by the author other
than for educational purposes and for reference under fair use doctrine.

All readers are encouraged to go to a WW Workshop or the WW website for actual WW information
and to also enter the listed ingredients of my recipes themselves into the Recipe Builder. Point
values for certain ingredients change and are updated periodically by WW®, which may
change the point values we are suggesting to be accurate for our recipes at this time.

This guide is in **NO WAY** meant to be a replacement for the WW Program. It is merely
developed and intended for use as a collection of privately developed recipes,
designed to complement the instructional materials and resources
provided by WW to its members... BECAUSE WW IS AWESOME!

Any non-generic recipes within this guide were developed by me.
All Point values were determined by entering the ingredients, measurements and
servings into the Recipe Builder within the WW mobile App that is only
available to paying members of the system. I strongly encourage anyone interested
in developing a healthier lifestyle to join and follow the strategies for healthy living
provided by Weight Watchers International (WW®).

All use of the terms Weight Watchers, WW, Point, Points, Smart Points, SP's and Freestyle
in the following cookbook are used SOLELY for reference purposes,
as is appropriate and allowed under fair use doctrine.

This publication is dedicated to my loving wife, whom I will never deserve. You have stood by me, a steadfast rock, weathering every storm and tempest that we've faced. You have supported and encouraged me during every phase of the past 18 years, and have held my hand through the darkest nights. Thank you for saying "Yes" all those years ago and for putting up with me ever since. On a positive, at least there's a whole lot less of me for you to put up with now.

- Daniel

Pesto Sauce
Low Point Sauces - pg. 75

Red Enchilada Sauce - pg. 77
Fat Free Cheese Hack - pg. 37
Low Point Masa (for tortillas & tamales) - pg. 38-39

How To Make Fat Free Cream Cheese Substitute
Foundation Recipes - pg. 36

How To Make Low Point Fresh Pasta
Foundation Recipes - pg. 40-43

Is This A Cookbook?

Yes… and No. When I published the first edition of this cooking guide, back in December 2018, it was born out of a desire to try and help absolutely every single person in-program that I could. Every single day I'd log into Connect and read about people struggling, not knowing how to work the system, or unaware of all of the awesome little tips and tricks that we all use in our food prep. I thought that it would be a tremendous service, if I could try and compile all the food hacks and cooking cheats that I'd learned about, then put them into one place.

Most everything in this book is a direct request from one person or another in Connect. The tutorial for low point pasta? It came from seeing people constantly talking about how much they missed eating REAL pasta, because of how high it is in calories, carbs and points. Every single one of the 31 sauces in the Sauce section, was specifically requested by different members in Connect. The Recipe Builder tutorial came from recognizing the need for it, when night after night, people talked about how much they missed having food they loved pre-program, followed by saying they'll never be able to make family-favorite meals again.

The original Cooking Guide that I published in 2018 had such an overwhelming response. I never would have imagined that there was such an insane desire and need for something like this. All of the famous food bloggers and chefs… they all pump out cookbooks like a conveyor belt. Here's the thing though… ever heard that age-old adage, "Give a man to fish and you feed him for a day. Teach him to fish and you feed him for life."? Well… same principle. My entire purpose for writing and putting this together is to TEACH YOU to cook differently, on your own, without me. I don't want to teach you to just blindly follow my recipes. I want to SHOW YOU how to use my basic principles to get those gears turning in your head, so that you have the light switch turn on and YOU start hacking down regular recipes like I do. I want to embolden you, and get you to start thinking outside of the box, with recipes and ingredients. I want you to not NEED my recipes after a while.

I want you to finish reading through this cooking guide and feel empowered in your kitchen. I want you to try out new techniques and ingredients that you wouldn't have before. I want you to close this baby, open up the Recipe Builder and start playing around with modifying recipes, like a rockstar. Between my Foundation recipes and the low point sauce recipes, combined with the 6 pages of food hack and ingredient swap ideas… you should be able to look at almost ANY recipe, from any website or magazine, then start dropping points like Godzilla drops skyscrapers in Tokyo. Now, let's get cooking!

Note: How To Read Measurements In This Guide

There has been some confusion on Connect from some folks about how to read the way that I write my measurements. So here goes:

1-1/4 = 1 and 1/4 of something, as in 1 and 1/4 teaspoons
2-1/2 = 2 and 1/2 of something, as in 2 and 1/2 teaspoons
3-3/4 = 3 and 3/4 of something, as in 3 and 3/4 teaspoons

Points: (G) (B) (P)

	G	B	P
1 serving =	1	0	0
2 servings =	2	1	1
3 servings =	3	1	1

Alright, I figured that I might as well explain this graphic to the left, because you're going to be seeing it on every recipe. This shows how many points each recipe has, for each serving, on each plan.

Think of it like the game "Battleship". On the left is how many servings, and on the right is how many points for that serving. It is NOT cummulative. In this case, if you want 3 servings of the Green recipe, it is 3 points. You do not add the 1st serving, with the 2nd serving, then the 3rd serving. Look at the serving #, then go across to the right program's color. That's how many points it is for that 1 serving. 1 serving of purple is 0 points, 2 servings of Blue is 1 point.

Table of Contents

2020 | Cookbook: Volume 1 - Second Edition
Cooking Strategies for the WW Green, Blue & Purple Plans.

Fresh, Home Made Pasta, with White Wine Butter Garlic Sauce

Introduction

Just who is this mythical, unibrowed recipe ninja, known simply as…. The Daniel?

My Cooking Philosophy

Trying to help you all understand the reasoning behind why I cook the way that I do, as well as why I feel it's so important to use the Recipe Builder to cut points and calories from recipes

Important Kitchen Gadgets

This is geared towards the newer cooks in the kitchen, I want to highlight a few of the kitchen gadgets that I use a LOT in my cooking, that make things so much easier

Ingredient Swaps & Substitutions

Now we're getting into the nitty gritty. Six pages of suggestions, tips and ideas for food substitutions. These pages are filled with ideas for swapping out high point, high calorie, high fat ingredients in recipes.

Recipe Builder Tutorial

This is the most important part of the entire book. This 6 page section will walk you through, step by step, the process of entering recipes into the app's recipe builder. You'll also be taken through 4 exercises showing how I'd modify high point recipes to get them lower in points and calories.

Eggs Benedict with Low Point Hollandaise & Smoked Salmon

Foundation Recipes

Recipes for 24 low point "foundations" that act as the building blocks for meals, such as: Lower point & calorie Masa for tortillas and tamales, fresh pasta, yeast pizza dough, slider/burger buns, and much more. This section ALSO features ground meat seasonings for chorizo, italian sausage, breakfast sausage and more…

Low Point Sauces

Recipes for 31 delicious sauces that are packed with flavor and are sure to elevate your dishes

Bonus Section - Holiday Dishes!!

Seeing that this is coming out in the Fall, I thought it'd be extremely helpful to include recipes for a few dishes that could help get you through the Holidays in one piece. Show that Turkey who's boss!

Closing Thoughts & Acknowledgements

My final ramblings, hopefully not toooo incoherant, as well as shout outs to some of the folks that helped get this crazy train rollin' down the tracks.

Recipe Index

Even though I like make you folks wave your first in the air, trying to find recipes… I figured I'd try to be helpful this time around

I WANT YOU
TO START COOKING
LOWER POINT & CALORIE MEALS

Introduction

Alright, for you folks that already have "The 2019 Low Point Cooking Guide" or follow me on Connect, this is going to be preeeeetty repetitive. Sorry *shrugs*
This is mainly for the folks that don't know me yet.

Hi there, my name is Daniel, but most of you know me from **WW Connect** as dhallakx7. As of the writing of this cookbook, I'm a 42-year-old stay at home dad to my 2 special needs kidlettes, Rachel (Autistic) and Jesse (Down Syndrome). Prior to this, I worked as a Graphic Designer & Web Developer for a really great company. I had just received a promotion, but when Jesse was born preemie and his diagnosis was finally confirmed, our priorities had to change, so I became Mr. Mom.

I still remember the night in 3rd grade when I turned from liking food, to wanting to gorge on food. My best friend Bart and I went to a high school soccer game with my older brother. At that game I saw something that I'd never seen before. A food vendor showed up in the bleachers pushing a food cart. He was using it to make hot, sugar coated mini cake donuts, fresh to order. I remember running down to that cart with my friend, looking at the fresh donuts, then immediately running up to my brother and asking for the money to buy some... then to buy some more... then to buy some more. And that's where it started.

I spent the better part of the next 30 years going from "husky" to overweight, eventually becoming heavy enough to be classified as obese. I only went swimming 3 or 4 times in the past 25 years out of shame for how I looked. I would make excuses not to see friends who were visiting from out of town, whom I hadn't seen in years. Heck, I wouldn't even change in the same room as my wife because I was

The new and improved 2019 Dad Bod GTO. Now available with dual child carriers, improved mileage and extended warranty

embarrassed about my body. Yet, did it make me want to change and lose weight? Nope, I figured it wasn't worth it.

In order to lose weight, I was going to be eating nothing but rice cakes and tasteless diet food. I would have to start going to the gym, running and stop eating all the foods that I loved to eat. People on diets are always so miserable and complain about what they can't eat, how their diet de jour doesn't allow them to have sugar, or they are cutting all carbs, or they are doing "cleanses" or whatever insane dietary deprivation is the current trend. Why in the heck would I want to do that? I'd rather be fat and eating than be skinny and surviving on rice cakes, bean curd and sadness. But, when I finally hit my mental rock bottom, I stumbled upon an article online late at night. It was written by a female blogger who tried Weight Watchers for one month without doing any exercise and without giving up eating regular food. She ended up losing 5 pounds over the course of the month without working out, while still eating normal foods and staying within her Weight Watchers daily allotment of "Smart Points". I figured it was worth a shot as I had no

Don't let food manipulate you, learn to manipulate your food

Rethink How You Cook

o Lower the fat, calories, sugar and carbs of foods, by swapping out high fat & calorie ingredients.
o Lose weight, by turning high fat & calorie food that you love, into a leaner and healthier dish.
o Retrain your brain to automatically think of ingredient substitutions, making this journey livable, sustainable, and enjoyable with GREAT food.

Cont.

Introduction

desire to stop eating normal food and no desire to exercise (at that time). The first few weeks were difficult but manageable. I was losing weight, I wasn't working out, but dear Lord, there was so much food that I missed eating that I couldn't have because it was so high in points. Then it happened... I found the "recipe builder' tool, within the WW mobile phone App, that pretty much changed everything.

I immediately realized the full possibilities the tool offered. I bought a cooking magazine from the grocery store, that had a recipe on the cover for a skillet full of baked rolls covered in tons of cheese, marinara sauce, pepperoni and Italian sausage. The type of meal there is NO WAY you could ever eat on Weight Watchers and stay within your points.

I scoured Connect for ingredient swap ideas and even came up with a few ideas of my own. I started swapping out regular cheese for fat free cheese and mixed in some plain yogurt for added creaminess. I adjusted spice amounts, checked how much wine I could cut with water to reduce the points and still taste it in a sauce. I tried getting as creative as I possibly could to make the skillet as low fat and low calorie as possible. Each time I did that with a new recipe, it became more and more fun, like challenging myself to solve a difficult puzzle. Now I can look at almost any recipe and think of ways to almost immediately start cutting the calories, while retaining the flavor.

Now, I absolutely LOVE doing this. I wake up every day, genuinely looking forward to "what am I going to try and make today?" I love logging in to the WW mobile app to check and see if there's anyone that needs a question answered, or needs help with a recipe... I love getting tagged by people who are looking for help.

After being stuck in a house, changing diapers, vacuuming, or being a taxi all day... getting to interact with adults who value you and want to chat, even if it's digitally, is such a relief.

My Food Philosophy

You might be tempted to gloss over this and go straight to the recipes, but please don't. This is very important. Before you dig into these recipes and get an extremely confused look as you exclaim, "Why in the good Lord's name is he doing this and (or)that?..." You need to understand the reason for my mad scientist-ness.

The most important factor is that I love, love, love to try challenging myself to think of new ways to do things. My primary goal in anything that I make is to make it taste great while cutting down the fat, calories and WW Points. My goal is to turn EVERYTHING into an ultra low calorie version of itself. Cooking with that mindset is what allowed me to lose so much weight, so fast, without ANY exercise... and while still eating well. I didn't even go for 1 single walk during my march from start, till I hit my goal weight. I dropped weight like a brick, while eating lasagna, pasta dishes, casseroles and desserts. My style of cooking relies upon the principle of "Calorie Density."

The basic principle of Calorie Density is that by modifying recipes to be lower in calories, you can consume the EXACT SAME AMOUNT OF FOOD, by weight, as someone else, but with a drastic reduction in the amount of calories you consume in a day. It's like choosing to eat a 1 pound Lean Cuisine dinner, while your buddy eats a 1 pound Stouffers dinner. You're both eating the same exact amount of food... but your meal is leaner and healthier.

When you're trying to eat healthier and lose weight, do you reach for "Hungry Man XL" frozen dinners, or do you reach for "Healthy Choice" Steamers"? You eat the Healthy Choice meal because it's a responsible amount of food, but lighter in fat, calories, carbs and sugars. It doesn't all have to be crazy food swaps, even something as simple as using a few shots of cooking spray to coat chicken, rather than the two teaspoons a recipe might call for, might SEEM insignificant... but those 2 points AREN'T just "points". We just removed 80 calories of fat from our dish. We're still having the exact same meal... just smarter. 80 calories might not sound like much, but do that across every meal, every day, all year, and you've cut tens of thousands of calories, fat and sugars... while still eating the same food, just... healthier.

It's weight loss 101, folks. No matter what fad diet you follow, they all have the same basic principle. If you eat more calories than your body uses in a day... you're going to gain weight. Most people try to cut calories by starving themselves. THAT slows your metabolism and makes you actually gain weight once you start eating again. BUT..... by manipulating your food to so that you eat just as much, just as often, but at half the calories. There is no starving, no slowing of your metabolism... you're still eating like a normal person, just leaner.

That's the basic principle for why I go crazy-mad-scientist in the kitchen, to the extent that I do. It allows me to have a larger portion size, even seconds, most of the time... and still able to lose or maintain my weight. While other people are constantly being told "Just eat the normal, full fat, full calorie dish... just have a much smaller portion... this is a lifestyle!", I say forget that. Who wants a "lifestyle" that revolves around having fat-filled little hockey puck sized "responsible" entrees and desserts. I don't want to feel like I'm on a diet or have to eat a portion of food that's sized for a toddler.

This cooking guide, which is the Second Edition of my Guide, originally published in 2018, is a treasure trove of tutorials, tips, and building block recipes meant to teach you to start manipulating your recipes, using my food hacks and tricks. I want to teach you to look at ANY recipe, no matter how indulgent and fatty, and KNOW that you can rework it. I want you to feel the freedom of knowing that YOU control your food, it's not in control of you.

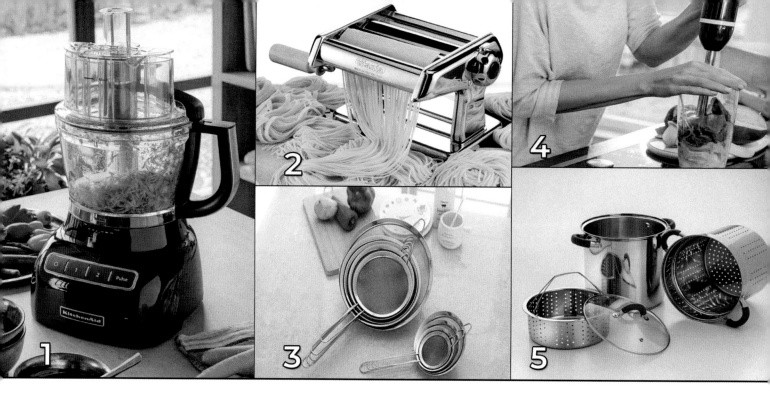

For most of you folks that cook a lot and have spent years trying new things in the kitchen, these Gadgets & Gizmos are nothing new to you. But this particular page is directed more towards people who aren't as comfortable in the kitchen yet and are wondering what some of the things are that I mention a lot in my posts. I've often heard people say "what's a food processor,?" or "Immersion Blender?" Well I thought it'd be a good use of a page to point out what some of the primary things are that I use, and what their purpose is, for the newer cooks in the kitchen.

1. Food Processor

Think of a food processor of a giant, wide bottomed blender. There are quite a few dips and dressings that are in this cookbook that rely heavily on using a food processor. ESPECIALLY the guacamole and the hummus. Sweet Lord in Heaven, it's worth it to get an inexpensive food processor for the Hummus recipe alone.

You don't need to buy an expensive model. Even just an inexpensive one from Big Lots will do the job. It is a necessity for a couple of the recipes.

2. Pasta Makers

Fresh pasta, if made the way that I teach, is lower in points and calories than store bought dried pasta. The Foundation recipe section has a great step by step tutorial for making fresh pasta. Making your pasta in the way that I show in this guide, will allows you to make a pasta sheet, half the size of a sheet pan, for just 3 points.

3. Wire Strainers

These are used EXTENSIVELY in my cupcake and cake recipes, as well as in a few of the dips and sauces. You don't need an expensive set. I got mine at the 99 cent store and they've lasted for years.

4. Immersion Blender

YOU NEED THIS IN YOUR LIFE! It's essentially a small blender at the end of a stick. It is used in all of the recipes for my "creamy" dressings. Throw all of the dressing ingredients into the cup, use the immersion blender... you have dressing in 15 seconds. You can also use a regular blender as well, but it takes up a lot more counterspace. You can purchase an inexpensive one at walmart for $20. You don't need the ultra expensive brands that have more gadgets than a swiss army knife.

5. Stock Pot with Steamer Inserts

This sounds like something that would be crazy expensive, but I've seen them at Ross and Marshalls for $20-$30. They are so worth it. I use the deep insert to steam cakes inside of a Corningware ceramic round dish, as well as using it to steam my Weight Watchers friendly Tamales (pg 98) and Seafood Boils. I use the shallower steamer insert to steam 2 ingredient dough for Asian steamed buns, bahn mi bites and stuffed tamale ball appetizers. .There are crazy ridiculous big brand ones, but honestly, you can find a $40 one on Amazon that will last you forever.

You may be fighting the thought of that purchase, but once you make the tamales and steamed cake, you won't regret it.

The Fat Free "cheese hack" lets you have melty cheese for an entire pan of Lasagna for only 4sp in total

Ultra Low Point Pie Crust

Low Point & Carb Breading

13sp
Fresh Pasta

13sp
Store Bought

Swaps, Hacks, & Tips

Ideas for Swapping Ingredients in Recipes

Retrain Your Brain

If you think about it, the primary purpose of the Recipe Builder in the Weight Watchers App is to make us WANT to cook our food with less fat, calories, sugars and carbs. Every time you lower the point value of a recipe with ingredient swaps, you have cut 1 or all those 4 things.

Lowering the Points for Butter

Molly McButter Fat Free Sprinkles
This stuff is amazing. It's a fine powder that dissolves perfectly in liquids and gives the flavor and color of butter. You can use up to 1 tablespoon for 0 points. It's a go-to staple in my kitchen for sauces.

I Can't Believe It's Not Butter- Light
Don't get one of the other types of I Can't Believe It's Not Butter spreads. Make sure you get the one that says "Light" and scan it to make sure. It is a butter flavored spread that can be used perfectly in place of butter, but at a fraction of the points. A ¼ cup is only 6sp, while ¼ cup of real butter is 20sp. Perfect for when you MUST use butter, but need to reduce the points, calories, and fat.

ULTRA Low Point Pie Crusts

Kellogg's All-Bran or Fiber One
Traditionally, for a pie crust you'd use crushed up graham crackers. But the amount of graham crackers and butter for that is around 36-46sp. If you put All-Bran or Fiber One cereal in a food processor with a little bit of FF Yogurt and some 0 point sweetener (monkfruit, swerve, etc.) and sugar free maple syrup, along with some Molly Mcbutter or I Can't Believe It's Not Butter Light, you can make an entire pie crust for only 7sp.

Yogurt For Oil In Cake Mixes

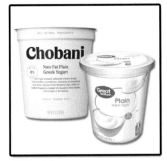

Fat Free Plain Greek Yogurt
Yogurt is a good substitute for mayo and sour cream in most recipes, though it can easily curdle when introduced into sauces or hot liquids. Let the liquids or dishes cool a bit before you bring the yogurts up to temperature and mix them in. You can also mix Greek into high point salad dressings to get more servings and lower the points.

Fat Free Plain Yogurt I personally prefer to use Plain Yogurt as a substitute for sour cream, rather than Greek Yogurt, as it is thinner and more closely resembles the viscosity of oil.

Yogurt for Mayo and Dairy

Fat Free Greek & Plain Yogurt
Along with being used to sub for oil in baking, you can also use FF Yogurts to sub for mayo, sour cream, milk and even cream in different applications. Use it instead of cream or milk with mashed cauliflower, sub it for mayo in dips and dressings and with a few tests, you can even use it as a sub for cream in certain sauces. Just don't add it to very hot liquids and dishes without tempering it or it will curdle.

Substititions for Honey

How To Swap Out Bee Puke.
As delicious and complex a flavor as honey is, it is also very high in points and sugars. There are a few options for getting around it though. #1, *Sugar Free Pancake Syrup.* The flavor profile is different, but it is sweet, thick and a lot lower in points. #2, *Sugar Free Imitation Honey.* You can purchase it online, pretty cheap through Walmart. However, it is barely lower point than real honey and only has 10 less calories per Tablespoon, still a good option for diabetic folks though. #3, *Honey flavored Extract.* Just like Vanilla extract, but made to taste like honey. You can purchase it cheap online. I like to bring 1/2 cup of water, 1-1/2 tsp of cornstarch, 1 tsp of the extract and some sweetener to a low boil for 3-4 minutes. Once cooled, you get 1/4 cup of thick "honey".

Low Point Breading for Meats & Veggies

Non Traditional Breading Ideas
Store bought breadcrumbs pack a pretty high point punch. Want lower point bread crumbs? Try Mashed potato flakes, or crushed rice krispies, whole wheat cheerios, or corn flakes. There's also the obvious fix... buy low point bread, like Sara Lee 45 calorie, 1 point slices, then make your own crumbs.

Melting Fat Free Cheese Hack

Fat Free Mozzarella & Cheddar
This is a game changer. Using this hack you can "cheese" an entire pan of Lasagna with 2 cups (really 3) of melty Mozzarella for only 4sp. The biggest problem with FF cheese is that it doesn't melt. That problem is solved if you mix it with a bit of FF plain (or Greek) yogurt. Sounds wrong, but it's amazing. Mix any amount of Kraft (or other brand) Fat Free shredded cheese with about 3/4 as much FF plain yogurt and mix until it forms a cheesy goopy mixture. Use it on Chicken Parmesan, Lasagnas or stuffed in a chicken breast. It works like a charm.

Fresh Pasta to the Rescue

Don't Give Up Your Pasta!!!!
Unless you're on the Purple plan, pasta is your sad emoji. Yes, there's store bought pasta that's crazy-high in carbs and points, not to mention it's a pain in the booty to portion easily. Well, rejoice! Using the recipe on page 40-43, I'll show you how real, fresh pasta is lower in carbs, calories, points and is easier to portion than store bought pasta. Not to mention it tastes 10,000 times better than that dried stuff you buy for $1.

Osp Italian Sausage, Chorizo, & More

with Seasoned Ground Turkey
Don't get me wrong, I like beef... but ground beef is expensive, is high in points and sits in my gut like a brick. I've spent a LOT of time developing ground meat seasonings (pg's 26-31), that allow you to have low point, calorie and fat, chorizo, italian sausage, bratwurst and more. It's an incredibly tasty way to cut calories from your meals, without really losing much in the way of that dish's traditional flavor. Give the recipes a try, you won't regret it.

Quickly "Ripen" Yellow Bananas

Sweeten up those baked goods
Ever tried to make a banana bread or another baked item that calls for "very ripe" bananas, but all that you have are the firm yellow ones without a fleck of black on them? Here's a quick fix. Throw the firm bananas (in their skin) onto a pie pan, and bake them at 325 degrees for 15-20 minutes, then let it cool.

Pudding without Milk or Yogurt

Thickening without Dairy or Fat
It's one of the annoying things about pudding, it just won't thicken if you use water, soy milk, almond milk or whatever. Well, that's not the case. If you use HALF as much of a non fatty fluid as the directions call for milk, it works. If you want it to have the consistency of regular pudding, use 1 cup of COLD liquid in place of the 2 cups milk. If you are wanting it thick enough to where it can keep its shape for a frosting, use 2/3 cup. So, use (1) 1oz packet of instant pudding and 1 cup cold water for pudding or 3/4 to 2/3 cup for frosting.

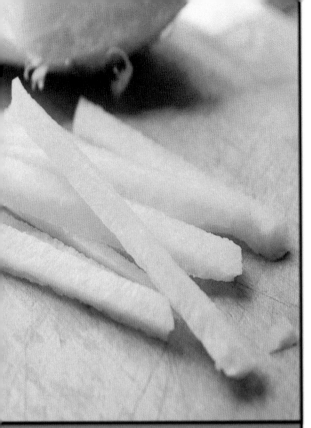

Jicama is a surprisingly good substitute for french fries

Research Tirelessly

Other than telling you to dig into the Recipe Builder, this is the best advice I can give you on this food journey. When it comes to ideas for food substitutions, the Internet is your friend. Most of the things that I've thought to try came from late night Google searches, trying to figure out how I could substitute or make lower versions of things.

THINK OUTSIDE THE BOX!! I didn't reinvent the wheel with this stuff, I just pulled it from somewhere else and Weight Watcher-ized it. A prime example is the Low Point Pie Crust. I found the idea for that on a Diabetic cooking site because they have to drastically reduce their sugar intake. When I wanted to find 0sp potato alternatives for French fries, I figured that I should look on "low carb" cooking forums and sites. The goal of this system is to retrain us to make healthier food choices, and the goal of the recipe builder is to subtlety push us towards making our foods as healthy (and lower in points) as possible.

Challenge yourself to think. Find or try new ways to substitute ingredients. Then you'll be able to have pretty much anything, guilt free, with a little bit of time in the kitchen.

Potato Substitutes

0sp Potato Alternatives

A few months back I got determined to have a big bowl of nacho cheese fries. Only one problem, potatoes are very high in points. I spent days combing through low carb cooking sites and compiled a short list of what people on low carb diets use to sub for potatoes. I then went about trying out the different veggies. The following are listed in no particular order.

Rutabaga & Radish

Rutabaga is a root vegetable that falls into the same family as broccoli, brussel sprouts and kale. Once it's washed and peeled, a rutabaga's orange flesh is similar in texture and flavor to a turnip. As for Radish, you normally only see them as a raw garnish. In their raw form, they are bitter and spicy. However, when you cook them, they mellow out and take on a more potato-like texture. Plus they are full of nutrients..

Celery Root (listed as "celeriac" in the App)

Celeriac has a mild celery flavor and is often used as a flavoring in soups and stews. It can also be used on its own, usually mashed, or used in casseroles, au gratins and baked dishes. It has a naturally savory flavor.

Jicama

Jicama resembles a large light-brown colored turnip. The white, creamy interior has a very crisp texture somewhat similar to a firm apple or raw potato. Cooking jicama or serving it raw are equally tasty ways to prepare this lightly sweet root

Pureed/Mashed Fruit & Veggies in Cake

More alternatives to oil in baking

As well as using fat free plain yogurt like we mentioned earlier, no sugar added and pureed fruits and vegetables are perfect 1:1 swaps in baking for most, if not all, of the recommended liquid ingredients listed on boxed cake mixes. Make sure to scan labels first though, as some brands DO add sugar.

DIY Self Rising Flour

Perfect for Gluten Free folks

Members with Gluten sensitivities have a rough time with a lot of recipes, especially the 2 ingredient dough that we all know and love. Simply add 1 1/2 teaspoons of baking powder and 1/4 teaspoon of salt to every 1 cup of WHATEVER flour you would like to use. Whether it's gluten free, whole wheat, cornmeal or any type of flour you want. Simply use that formula and you'll have your own self rising flour.

Replacing Heavy Cream

Thickening soups, sauces, gravies

One of the most annoying things about "normal" recipes is how much heavy cream goes into EVERYTHING. I don't use cream or half and half in ANY of my recipes. How do I thicken sauces and soups? I use cornstarch, heated with almond, nonfat, or low carb milk. You can also try, powdered milk, silken tofu, potato flakes, xanthum gum, tempered Greek yogurt... heck, you can even use canned pumpkin puree or blended white beans to act as a thickener agent. Ground oatmeal works on the Purple plan too.

Fat Free & Reduced Fat Cheeses

The Hard To Find Ingredient

It's obvious that you should swap full fat cheese for reduced fat cheese, however, there's another variety that you can try... if you can find it. Fat Free cheese.You can "cheese" an entire Lasagna with my fat free cheese hack for 4 points versus 19 points for reduced fat cheese. Kraft Fat Free cheese can usually be found, pretty reliably, at most Walmart grocery stores.

Flavored Popcorn Seasonings

They Ain't Just For Popcorn!!

Want a wide range of low calorie, low point, non traditional flavor seasonings that pack a TON of punch? Go the the popcorn aisle at the store and take a look at all the flavors of popcorn sprinkles. Scan them to see the points, but you can use them to flavor desserts, sauces, appetizers... there is a TON of different flavors and brands. My cheese sauce, later in the book, calls for Molly Mcbutter brand cheese powder. You can use one of these though. Every store has them.

Fat Free "Cream Cheese"

Seriously... it's simple

By using cheese cloth, or paper coffee strainers, to strain Greek yogurt overnight, it takes on the texture of softened cream cheese. On the Blue and Purple plans, it has absolutely no points, on Green, just count it as Greek. It can be used in spreads, dressings, dips and even frostings for cakes and cupcakes. An alternative for Green that I personally haven't tried, but have heard good things about, is to run fat free cottage cheese in a food processor to make it smooth, then strain it just like you would the Greek yogurt.

Flavored Cooking Sprays Instead of Oil

Obvious, but deserves a shout-out

I personally use a TON of butter flavored cooking spray. When seasoning raw meats, I hit both sides with butter flavored or olive oil flavored cooking spray to help flavor the meat. You can also use the butter spray on popcorn. Use the olive oil spray to lightly hit the top of homemade low point hummus or other dishes instead of drizzling olive oil on them. There are tons of ways to use flavored sprays as a seasoning.

Powdered Peanut Butter

Dehydrated and nearly Fat Free PB

Powdered peanut butter, regardless of the brand, is freaking awesome. You can mix it with water to rehydrate it for use as regular peanut butter or you can add the powder to recipes and baked goods to give a PB flavor without all the added mass, points, or stickiness. It's great in everything from smoothies to satay sauces, baking mixes or mixed with pudding or yogurt. The best part being that it's a fraction of the points of regular peanut butter. Allergic to peanuts? There's powdered Almond butter.

Dairy Free Yogurt Hack

Go Go Gadget, TOFU!

When I first started posting recipes for Greek yogurt based salad dressings, then began using strained Greek yogurt instead of Fat Free cream cheese in my frostings... people started asking about something I'd never thought of before. What to use instead of Greek, when you're allergic to dairy?

Greek yogurt is such a huge building block of so many things in system. 2 Ingredient dough, breakfast parfaits, using it in place of sour cream... heck, I even use it to replace Lard in my Tamales. It made me start looking around for an easy alternative. I found one, it works, but it's a bit unconventional. Tofu. Yup... that's right. It's readily available at grocery stores, inexpensive, and doesn't have a strong flavor (unlike Greek). It comes in different levels of firmness. Firm, which you can dent a Buick with. Semi or Medium Firm, which is like a cooled block of cream cheese, then Silken (or soft), which is almost like Plain yogurt.

I blend a 16 ounce block of semi firm tofu with 1/2 cup water, to make a viable replacement for Greek yogurt. It works for 2 ingredient dough and salad dressings. It does "tighten" up a bit in the fridge though, so add more water if necessary. If you want that tang that Greek has, add a splash of lemon juice. After you blend it, you can also strain it again, like my Fat Free "cream cheese", to use it in frostings. Does it taste the same as Greek? No, but it's a great alternative, if you have allergies. It works.

Laughing Cow Cheese Wedges

Low Point & Calorie Spread

I haven't personally used it, but so many people swear by these spreadable cheese wedges, that I HAD to include them. They are great as a 1 point cheesy snack, but their creamy consistency also makes it a great substitution for mayonnaise. You can mix it in with tuna or an egg salad sandwich, use it simply as a spread on toast or a bagel, or in an other application you might use light mayo or soft cream cheese.

DIY Low Point Brown Sugar Substitute

A Little Molasses Goes a Long Way

First off.... YES... I know that you can buy 0 point brown sugar substitutes. Popular ones are Lakonta brand "golden" monkfruit, Splenda makes an artificial brown sugar, Swerve, Sukrin Gold, there's a lot of them. However... I can't find them in the grocery stores by my house and I don't want to order them online.

Luckily there's an easy fix. Real brown sugar is simply regular sugar mixed with a little molasses. Well, if you have molasses and any type of sweetener, you can sub it in recipes. 1/4 tsp of molasses is 0 points. If I'm making a dish that calls for 1/4 cup or less of brown sugar, I'll use that much sweetener, then add the 1/4 tsp molasses to the dish. It tastes great. Feel free to use more, but adjust your points accordingly.

Substitutions For Food Allergies

Just a few to consider

I'm going to be mentioning a bunch of stuff in here, so let's quit with the bantering.
Allergic to peanuts but need a little peanut butter in a recipe? Puree some garbanzo beans. The flavor's a little different, but it'll work. If you can have sesame seeds, add up to 1/4 tsp sesame oil to the puree.

Allergic to eggs? replace 1 egg in a baked good with 1/4 cup of pumpkin puree or mashed banana. Add a little baking powder if you want to help add a little lift. Bob's Red Mill makes certified Gluten Free All Purpose Flour that already has xanthum gum and other binders in it to help fortify the flour. If you are making a Greek Yogurt based creamy dressing and are allergic to dairy, blend tofu with water. If you want to make one of my cake recipes, that are based on Pillsbury Sugar Free cake mixes, but you're allergic to gluten or splenda, "Swerve" makes a gluten free, sugar free cake mix, that is sweetened with erythritol. Also, "Namaste" brand baking mixes has a ton of ALL allergen free mixes, though they are a little higher in points (not sugar free).

Purple Plan Pasta & Flour Conundrums

Let the ridiculous WW-Math begin!!

As of today's date (11-14-19), there is one bit of nonsense in the Purple plan, that you can take liberties with until they clarify it.
Ok... whole wheat flour, garbanzo or chickpea flour, black bean flour... pretty much all flours have points. However, whole wheat, chickpea, black bean and pretty much ALL types of pasta NOT made from white flour... are all 0 points on the purple plan. 1 cup of whole wheat flour is 12 points. Use that 1 cup of flour with some eggs and baking powder to make bread? It's 12 points. Use that 1 cup of flour with eggs and NO baking powder to make fresh whole wheat pasta?... 0 points. Say whaaaaaa??? So, apparently on the purple plan, once you turn non-white flour... flour...into pasta, it magically loses all of its points. Make crackers or bread with it? It keeps them. So'ya know what I say? Take my fresh pasta recipe and substitute the all purpose flour with whole wheat flour. You may need to adjust the amount of liquid, because different flour types absorb water differently, but you Purple People Eaters can make your own fresh, delicious, 0 point pasta with my recipe and the 1 single flour swap. The funny thing is... you can bake my pasta dough to make whole wheat bread, by adding baking powder. It would have points, as bread. Boil it as pasta? Same calories, same carbs.... no points. Try wrapping your coconut around that one.

Stretch The Servings with Low Point Fillers

Recipe Building 101

Your recipe has a certain amount of points in it. If that recipe makes 2 servings, it'll be twice the points as if it made 4 servings. By bulking up a dish with 0 or low point vegetables or proteins (depending on your plan), you can drastically increase the servings and decrease the points. Pictured to the left, is my awesome pasta salad recipe. I use my Ricotta Gnocchi recipe for the pasta, use sliced, grilled chicken breast for the meat, have it loaded with a TON of roasted 0 point vegetables and wilted spinach, then I have it dressed with some of my low point roasted garlic and onion salad dressing. The points from the ricotta gnocchi get stretched out with a BUNCH more servings, by adding the vegetables and chicken. It stretches the 10 points of ricotta gnocchi and 2 points of my dressing to make enough pasta salad for (6) 1 cup servings. So that gives us an entire cup of freakin GOURMET gnocchi pasta salad, loaded with grilled vegetables, chicken, wilted spinach and creamy roased garlic and onion dressing... for just 2 points per serving... on the Blue and Purple plans anyways. It'd be more on Green, because of the added points for greek yogurt in the dressing and the chicken. But it'd still be amazingly low calorie, fat and point. Even if you're on #TeamItAintEasyBeingGreen.

There are many, many, many other tips, tricks, hacks and ideas for ingredient substitutions that I'd like to add into this section, but I just don't have the space. Maybe in the future, we can keep having people contribute ideas, then we can make a big multi-page, expanded download available on my site, for free.

Low-ish Point and Calorie Milk & Cream Alternatives

Because of calories and points, I don't really use regular milk or cream in ANYTHING. I pretty much use almond milk, soy milk, or CARBMaster brand (from Kroger stores) lactose free milk in everything. They are all extremely low in points and calories, but equally as important, they are all THICKER THAN REGULAR MILK, which makes them ideal for helping to thicken pudding and sauces.

My coconut cupcakes and cake, call for "coconut flavored beverage", rather than canned, Light coconut milk. I use Silk or So Delicious brands, because they are 2 points for an entire cup of thick and light coconut milk. If your local store doesn't have them (they can be found by the almond milk), you can most likely find an almond/coconut milk blend that you can use in its place. If you are allergic to nuts and can't use almond milk in one of my recipes that calls for it, use ANY low point and calorie milk you can find. Carbmaster is my top pick though.

Stevia, Truvia, Monkfruit & Erythritol-Based Sweeteners

Whether people agree with me or not about using them... I have absolutely no problem whatsoever with using Sweeteners. "They aren't natural!" There are plenty of natural sweeteners that are NOT white sugar. My personal favorite is Lakanto brand monkfruit. I have to warn you on one though... "Monkfruit In The Raw" brand is mixed with multidextrine, it has the worst artificial aftertaste ever, in my opinion. Putting "in the raw" behind monkfruit on that package, is horribly misleading. Organic Stevia is a 100% natural sweetener, that even the 2 old men from the muppets can't honestly complain about.

My primary reason for using them is calories. First and foremost, I am most concerned with using anything I can to cut calories from my recipes, without cutting flavor or portion sizes. Using sweeteners instead of sugar, if you have no food sensitivies to them, is a no brainer. 1 cup of sugar has nearly 800 calories... you'd be hard pressed to find any recipe for a sweet bread, pie, or cake, that doesn't require 2 cups of it. By contrast, an entire cup of most sweeteners has 0 calories. I didn't get fat by eating sweetener, and I'm not about to give up desserts or eat tiny portions.

Different Types of Thickeners

Though I must admit that in my recipes, I typically only use cornstarch, I wanted to make sure to point out other commonly available ingredients that you can also experiment with.
- Cornstarch: A little bit goes a long way. You can go up to 1-1/2 tsp of cornstarch for 0 points, and up to around 1 Tbsp for only 1 point. Dissolve it in a tiny bit of liquid, then heat it up in a sauce or soup and let it simmer for a few minutes. It will thicken the sauce and you won't need as much of it as you would flour. The typical ratio that I like to use, is 1-1/2 tsp of cornstarch for each 3/4 cup liquid to thicken. Cornstarch is also Gluten Free.
- Xanthum Gum: Thickens just as well as cornstarch, but it doesn't need to be heated. You can use it to thicken cold liquids, like salad dressings.
- Gelatine: Great for jellies, gravies, and clear glazes.
- Potato Starch: Works just as well as cornstarch, but some folks like it better.
- Guar Gum: I don't have much experience with it, but it's readily available at stores.

Ground Oatmeal

I haven't done this, because I'm still on the Blue plan, but folks in Purple have mentioned that they will crush and grind up oatmeal, then will use it in place of bread crumbs, or as a thickening agent, for 0 points.

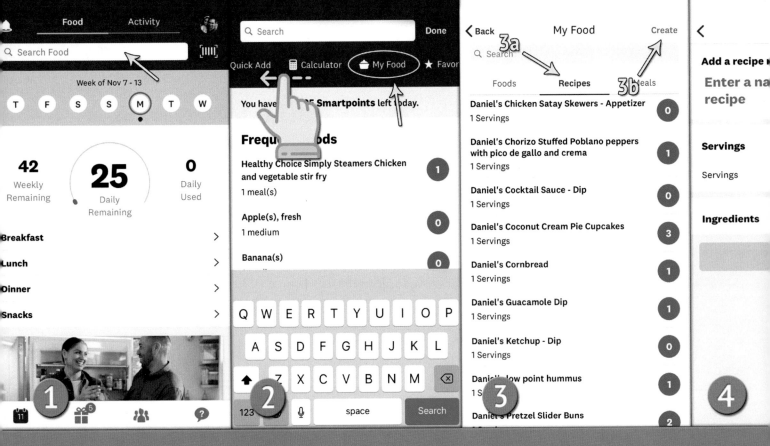

> "Teach a woman to fish and you feed her for a day, teach her to use the recipe builder and you've given her cheesecake. She'd rather have the cheesecake., trust me."
> - *The Book of Freestyle 11:11*

MASTERING

One of the first rewards I set for myself, was if and when I'd lose my first 20lbs, that I could have my mom's old chicken divan casserole Only one problem, I didn't have the recipe. So I went onto the food network's website and found the recipe from a very famous Southern Chef that loves her some butter, ya'll. I decided that I would use that for my Chicken Divan.

I opened up the App's Recipe Builder, entered in the recipe exactly as is, and couldn't believe that 1 single serving was 18 points. NO WAY was I going to eat that. I set about trying to make a healthier version and it completely changed everything. I was able to get that casserole down to 2 points per serving from her 18. It was my "Road to Damascus" moment with Weight Watchers.

I am going to do my absolute best in this section to help walk you through a step by step tutorial of how to do what I do with recipes I want to make WW Friendly. I'm going to talk you through how to enter that same chicken divan recipe that I found online, so that we can modify it together and you can learn to create, tweak and save your own recipes..

Although I'm going to be making this recipe in the Blue program, I will ALSO be showing how I'd tweak the same exact recipe in both the Green and Purple programs, as well as what the points would be in all 3 programs.

Recipe Builder 101

Alright folks, like I said, I'm going to do my best to help you get the fullest benefit out of the Recipe Builder. So, class is in session. For the benefit of the newer folks to the program, I'm going to type this out as if you have NEVER opened up the Recipe Builder in the app before.

NOTE: The process for adding recipes is very similar from your desktop computer on the WW website. On your computer click the "create" button to the right of the search bar on your desktop.

STEP 1: When you open the app on your mobile device, you'll be on your "my day" screen. Click the "search food" bar at the top.

STEP 2 & 3: On the next screen, swipe to the left, until you see "My Food", Click that. Next, When you get to the 3rd screen, (3a) click the *Recipes* tab, then (3b) "Create".

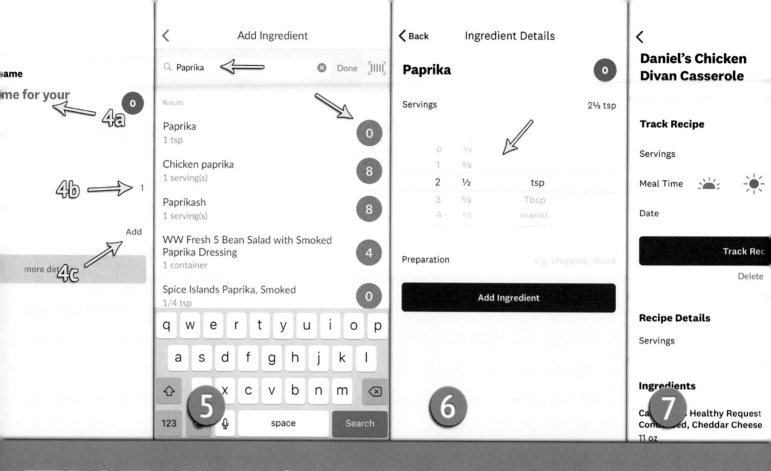

THE RECIPE BUILDER

Practicing the principles of this section will completely change your weight loss journey

STEP 4: Alright, now's where the fun begins. *(4a)* This is where you enter in the name of whatever you'd like your recipe to be called. *(4b)* is where you input the number of servings. The more servings you can get out of a dish, the further you stretch it's points and the fewer points per serving it becomes in most cases. If a dish has 30 points of ingredients in it and only 1 serving, then it's 30sp per serving. But if that recipe makes 6 servings then it's 5sp per serving. Lastly, *(4c)* is where the bulk of your time will be spent, adding ingredients. Pressing "add ingredient" takes you to...

STEP 5: Type in the name of an ingredient, in this case we'll search for Paprika. The spice paprika may not be the first thing that pops up and sometimes you need to scroll down to find the item for which you are looking. A prime example is Pepper. If you search to add Pepper you have to scroll down to find it between items like "black pepper chicken", "pepper jelly" and 30 other things. You'll often need to hunt for the ingredient you really want, but you'll eventually find it, or one like it that you can use. Here we'll select Paprika.

STEP 6: Now that you've selected Paprika as your ingredient to add, the program is going to have you enter how much of it you're going to use in the recipe. For a lot of spices, it doesn't matter. They stay "0" regardless of whether you use 1 tsp or 1/2 cup of it, there's no change. However, there

are a lot of spices and ingredients that scale up in points, depending on how much you use. This is where you get to really go to town with hacking recipes. But that's later. For now, we're just going to add in an entire recipe as is, with all of it's suggested ingredients, measurements and servings.

Recipe Exercise #1: (Full Fat Chicken Divan)

Create a new recipe and name it "AA - TEST RECIPE" so that it's easy to find and delete later. List it as having 8 servings and input the following ingredients and measurements. Do not choose "light sour cream" "reduced fat mayo" etc, use the full fat regular versions of everything. This exercise is to prove a point.

- 20oz Broccoli, cooked
- 6 cups shredded chicken, cooked
- 2 cans of condensed cream of mushroom soup
- 1 cup mayonnaise
- 1 cup sour cream
- 1 cup shredded cheddar cheese
- 1 tablespoon lemon juice
- 1 teaspoon curry powder
- 1/2 cup white wine
- 3/4 cup grated Parmesan
- 1/2 cup plain breadcrumbs
- 3 tablespoons butter

Recipe Builder

Let the Swapping Begin

For purposes of this tutorial, to make it as simple as possible, I am not going to be using things like the fat free cheese hack. We are going to use regular reduced fat cheese and other items that you can easily purchase from the store. So... let's dig in.

Pictured to the right is the in-app point values for the original full-fat Southern recipe. Your mission, should you choose to accept it, is to swap out and substitute these high point/fat/calorie ingredients, for lower point items that would work just as well.

STEP 1: First thing first. I decided that for me personally that I wanted the chicken, cheese and broccoli casserole to be extra cheesy. To further that goal and also to drop the points, I replaced the 2 cans of condensed cream of mushroom soup, with 1 can of "healthy request" condensed cheddar cheese soup. Why the can marked "healthy request?" It has 2 less points than the regular campbell's soup. That saved 9 points. Next, was the big fat-bomb, 1 cup of mayonnaise. I replaced it with 1 cup of greek yogurt. I already knew how I was going to make this work, so I left out the 1 cup of sour cream and instead, added 1/2 cup of water... trust me. I made up for the bulk by adding more broccoli, which adds more bulk for more servings. So, another 21 points gone. But... how are we going to thicken it without all the mayo? Cornstarch..... boom.

STEP 2: Let's get cheesy!!!!

The regular recipe calls for 1 cup of regular shredded cheddar cheese, and 3/4 cups of grated Parmesan cheese. We are going to get rid of that 28 points of combined full fat cheese. I want it cheesier, and meltier, so I replaced the grated parmesan with low fat mozzarella, which saved 4 points. Then swapped the full fat cheddar for reduced fat, saving another 6 points. The creaminess of the mozzarella, vs the original parmesan, will also help offset the lack of regular fatty creaminess from the mayo and sour cream. You can see how all of these subs are quickly making this casserole MUCH healthier, MUCH lower in points and MUCH lower in total fat and calories. But wait, we're not done yet, mis amigos!

STEP 3: Now we're coming into the home stretch, we're at the liquids. So we'll need water for the condensed soup, that's the water we mentioned earlier. Next is the lemon juice, which isn't a problem, then the white wine. Now, we just want the flavor of white wine in the dish. It can be subtle, it doesn't need to kick us in the face. So do you want a slight flavor?.. Try adding just 1 tablespoon of it in with water, want a little more? Add some white wine vinegar. The recipe asks for a 1/2 cup of white wine... we just cut another 4 points.

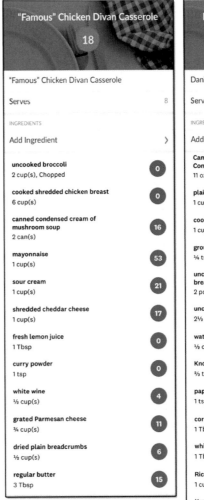

"Famous" Chicken Divan Casserole	18
"Famous" Chicken Divan Casserole	
Serves	8
INGREDIENTS	
Add Ingredient	>
uncooked broccoli — 2 cup(s), Chopped	0
cooked shredded chicken breast — 6 cup(s)	0
canned condensed cream of mushroom soup — 2 can(s)	16
mayonnaise — 1 cup(s)	53
sour cream — 1 cup(s)	21
shredded cheddar cheese — 1 cup(s)	17
fresh lemon juice — 1 Tbsp	0
curry powder — 1 tsp	0
white wine — ½ cup(s)	4
grated Parmesan cheese — ¾ cup(s)	11
dried plain breadcrumbs — ½ cup(s)	6
regular butter — 3 Tbsp	15

Original Recipe

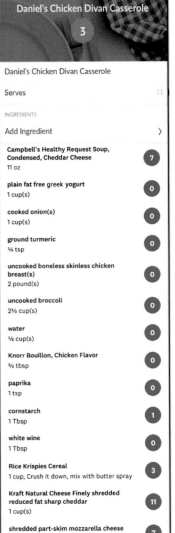

Daniel's Chicken Divan Casserole	3
Daniel's Chicken Divan Casserole	
Serves	11
INGREDIENTS	
Add Ingredient	>
Campbell's Healthy Request Soup, Condensed, Cheddar Cheese — 11 oz	7
plain fat free greek yogurt — 1 cup(s)	0
cooked onion(s) — 1 cup(s)	0
ground turmeric — ¼ tsp	0
uncooked boneless skinless chicken breast(s) — 2 pound(s)	0
uncooked broccoli — 2½ cup(s)	0
water — ½ cup(s)	0
Knorr Bouillon, Chicken Flavor — ⅔ tbsp	0
paprika — 1 tsp	0
cornstarch — 1 Tbsp	1
white wine — 1 Tbsp	0
Rice Krispies Cereal — 1 cup, Crush it down, mix with butter spray	3
Kraft Natural Cheese Finely shredded reduced fat sharp cheddar — 1 cup(s)	11
shredded part-skim mozzarella cheese — ¾ cup(s)	7

Revised Low Point Recipe

STEP 4: Now, because we have all of this liquid, we don't want our casserole to be runny, but we don't want to thicken it with a buttload of mayo, so what do we do? Cornstarch.... boom. Dissolve it with a tiny bit of water, then stir it in with the cheese sauce we'll make in the recipe (found in the Holiday side dishes). We're also going to be eliminating the butter, that's only used to mix with a ton of breadcrumbs, to sprinkle on top of the casserole. Instead, I'm going to crush up 1 cup of rice krispies and use those as the crumbs, it's lower points. Then, we'll put those in a bowl, spray them down with a 0 point amount of butter flavored cooking spray, toss it together, then use that as the topping.... End scene. *applause from the audience*

Note: If you are looking up your recipes through the WW website, the the database will often display the incorrect point value for the servings, it happens A LOT. I only check points for my recipes in the App., never on my PC. When you look up one of your recipes in the database, I'd highly suggest scroll down to 0 servings, then back to 1 serving. I have recipes that show up as 4 points for the first serving on green and purple, but 5 on blue. If I scroll to 0 servings then back to 1, it will correct to 4 points. Be advicsed.... the database is a tempermental, lying little hussie, sometimes. I also have recipes that only have 4 ingredient points, but when looked up through the website, will be 1 point per serving, even up to 200 servings, despite only having 4 points.

Plan Tweaks

GREEN PLAN

Daniel's Chicken Divan Casserole
4

Daniel's Chicken Divan Casserole	
Serves	11
INGREDIENTS	
Add Ingredient	>
Campbell's Healthy Request Soup, Condensed, Cheddar Cheese 11 oz	7
plain fat free greek yogurt 1 cup(s)	5
cooked onion(s) 1 cup(s)	0
ground turmeric ¼ tsp	0
uncooked boneless skinless chicken breast(s) 2 pound(s)	15
uncooked broccoli 2⅓ cup(s)	0
water ½ cup(s)	0
Knorr Bouillon, Chicken Flavor ⅔ tbsp	0
paprika 1 tsp	0
cornstarch 1 Tbsp	1
white wine 1 Tbsp	0
Rice Krispies Cereal 1 cup, Crush it down, mix with butter spray	3
Kraft Natural Cheese Finely shredded reduced fat sharp cheddar 1 cup(s)	11
shredded part-skim mozzarella cheese ¾ cup(s)	7

PURPLE PLAN

Daniel's Chicken Divan Casserole
3

Daniel's Chicken Divan Casserole	
Serves	11
INGREDIENTS	
Add Ingredient	>
Campbell's Healthy Request Soup, Condensed, Cheddar Cheese 11 oz	7
plain fat free greek yogurt 1 cup(s)	0
cooked onion(s) 1 cup(s)	0
ground turmeric ¼ tsp	0
uncooked boneless skinless chicken breast(s) 2 pound(s)	0
uncooked broccoli 2⅓ cup(s)	0
water ½ cup(s)	0
Knorr Bouillon, Chicken Flavor ⅔ tbsp	0
paprika 1 tsp	0
cornstarch 1 Tbsp	1
white wine 1 Tbsp	0
Rice Krispies Cereal 1 cup, Crush it down, mix with butter spray	3
Kraft Natural Cheese Finely shredded reduced fat sharp cheddar 1 cup(s)	11
shredded part-skim mozzarella cheese ¾ cup(s)	7

In this particular recipe, there isn't a DRASTIC difference in the points per serving, between plans. In most recipes that have multiple servings, going from Blue to Green will most likely go up a few points, but it won't be a crazy number. Likewise, in most cases, going from Blue to Purple with a recipe will either have the points per serving stay the same, or be reduced. That's due to the increased number of 0 point foods on Purple vs. Blue. If you are smart with your ingredient swaps and think outside of the box with substitutions, you really can have amazing and lighter version of the same dish, between all 3 different plans.

Green Changes:

As you can see, the points for certain ingredients change drastically from Blue to Green. The Greek yogurt and chicken get a lot of points, but for the most part, everything else in the recipe stayed the same, between the 2 plans. I did decide to try looking into lower point alternatives to Greek yogurt for the Green version though. I tried swapping it out with 1 cup of fat free cottage cheese, but though the cottage cheese is lower in points than Greek, the difference was so

minimal that the points per serving stayed at 4 for the first serving. It wasn't worth swapping out, though you can if you choose. The only other place to do an easy swap, would be using regular bread crumbs instead of crushed rice crispies. But you get more "crumbs" from 3 points of rice krispies than you do from 3 points of bread crumbs, so...It's fine as is.

Purple Changes:

With this particular recipe, there really isn't a whole lot of room for improvement, going from Blue to Purple. All of the foods that are 0 points on Blue, stay 0 points on Purple.

However, on purple, you COULD bulk this baby up and get even more servings out of it, which would lower the points per serving. There is a large number of whole grain foods that stay 0 points on Purple. You could add a cup or two of cooked wild rice into the casserole if you wish, that would definitely add servings and make for a much more hearty and filling dish, with no added points.

Ok... now that we have this basic intro out of the way, showing you how to input a recipe along with some simple ideas for how to cut the points, calories and fat down.... let's REALLY dive into it and get you to try it out. The next 2 pages are going to have exercises, that will help get your recipe-tweaking gears turning.

Builder Exercises

3 Regular Recipes and how I'd WW-ify them

My 3 point Chicken Tamales with Roasted Tomatillo Sauce

Yes, providing you with recipes and and explaining things is important, but without a doubt, THIS section is the most important part of this entire book. Helping to get you to start seeing just how easy it is for YOU, on your own, without me, to start creating healthier versions of your favorite fatty foods, is the most important thing that I can possibly do. I want to help you get to where you can just LOOK at a regular recipe and start disecting it, without even realizing you're doing it.

It takes a little practice, so I'd recommend looking at regular recipes online, that look like delicious, ultra unhealthy comfort food. Enter that recipe into the recipe builder... then start playing with it and swapping ingredients to see what you can get it down to. The more you practice, the better you get.

In these following 2 pages, I'm going to type out 3 regular recipes that I found online for traditional comfort dishes Then I'll explain how I'd knock them down. This is just an exercise, these are not actual finished/modified recipes. There are no listed steps or cooking instructions. This is just how I would modify the ingredients in the NORMAL recipes, that I found online. The listed points, are assuming the recipes are being built on the Blue plan.

Recipe Exercise #1

Green Chili Chicken Tamales
Servings: 8
Points: **12 points per tamale**

Ingredients: 99 total ingredient points

Filling: (36 points)
- 2 lb   Boneless, Skinless Chicken Thighs - **19sp**
- 1/4 cup   Olive Oil- **17sp**
- 1 lb   Tomatillos- **0sp**
- 1/2 tsp   Salt - **0sp**
- 1/4 tsp   Pepper - **0sp**
- 1/2 tsp   Cumin - **0sp**
- 1/2 tsp   Chili Powder - **0sp**
- 1 medium Onion - **0sp**
- 1   Jalapeno Pepper - **0sp**
- 1/2 lb   Poblano Peppers - **0sp**

Masa - Tamale Dough: (63 points)
- 2 cups   Masa Harina Corn Flour - **24sp**
- 1-1/2 cup Water
- 1/2 cup   Lard - **39sp**
- 1/2 tsp   Salt - **0sp**

WHAT WOULD I DO? *(with basic swaps)*:
Modified Points: 3 points per Tamale, on the Blue plan
(minus 75 total ingredient points)

Filling: (-36 ingredient points)
- Cook, then shred, boneless skinless chicken breasts, rather than chicken thighs. I'd then simmer them in the roasted & pureed green chili/tomatillo sauce. *(-19sp)*
- Use 0 point cooking spray instead of 1/4 cup of olive oil, to cook the chicken and roast the vegetables. *(-17sp)*

Masa: *(-39 ingredient points)*
- Use 1/2 cup of fat free Greek yogurt, rather than Lard, in the Masa. I'd also add 2 tsp of baking powder. It makes the tamales very soft and fluffy. *(-39sp)*

I actually HAVE made this. I even posted a video in Connect and on Youtube showing how to make them. In Connect, search **#dhallaktamales**. You can also find my video for my 0 point roasted tomatillo sauce and my 3 point tamales in my Youtube channel, **The Guilt Free Gourmet.**

Recipe Exercise #2

Old Fashioned Chicken Pot Pie
Servings: 6
*Points: **20 points per serving (Blue)***

Ingredients: 119 total ingredient points
Filling: (35 points)
- 1/3 cup   Butter - *27sp*
- 1/3 cup   All Purpose Flour - *4sp*
- 1 medium   Garlic Clove, minced - *0sp*
- 1/2 tsp   Salt - *0sp*
- 1/4 tsp   Pepper - *0sp*
- 1-1/2 cups Water - *0sp*
- 2/3 cup   Whole Milk - *4sp*
- 2 tsp   Chicken Bouillon Granules - *0sp*
- 2 cups   Cooked Boneless Chicken Breast, Cubed - *0sp*
- 1 cup   Frozen Mixed Vegetables - *0sp*

Crust: (84 points)
- 1-2/3 cups All Purpose Flour - *21sp*
- 2 tsp   Celery Seed - *0sp*
- 8 oz   Cream Cheese, cubed - *36sp*
- 1/3 cup   Cold Butter - *27sp*

WHAT WOULD I DO? *(with basic swaps):*
Modified Points: 5 points per serving (Blue)
(minus 89 total ingredient points)

Filling: *(-25 ingredient points)*
- Replace Butter with I Can't Believe It's Not Butter "Light" *(-19sp)*
- Use 1 Tbsp Cornstarch instead of the All Purpose Flour *(-3 points)*
- Use Almond Milk instead of whole milk *(-3 points)*

Crust: *(-64 ingredient points)*
- Use 1-1/2 cup portion of Yeast Pizza Dough (pg. 52) as the crust for the pot pie, it's not as traditional, but it's a lot healthier *(-64sp)*
  (Use whole wheat flour to make the pizza crust, on Purple, and it'll be even lower)

Recipe Exercise #3

"Healthy" Slow Cooker Meatloaf
Servings: 8
*Points: **9 points per serving (Blue)***

Ingredients: 69 total ingredient points
Filling: (54 points)
- 1/2 cup   Tomato Sauce - *0sp*
- 2 large   Eggs, beaten - *0sp*
- 1/4 cup   Ketchup - *3sp*
- 1 tsp   Worcestershire Sauce - *0sp*
- 1 small   Onion, chopped - *0sp*
- 1/3 cup   Crushed Saltines (10 crackers) - *4sp*
- 3/4 tsp   Garlic, minced - *0p*
- 1/4 tsp   Seasoning Salt - *0sp*
- 1-1/2 lbs. 90% Lean Ground Beef - *30sp*
- 1/2 lb.   Reduced-Fat Pork Sausage - *17sp*

Sauce: (15 points)
- 1/2 cup   Ketchup - *7sp*
- 3 tbsp   Brown Sugar - *8sp*

WHAT WOULD I DO? *(with basic swaps):*
Modified Points: 0 points per serving (Blue)
(minus 61 total ingredient points)

Filling: (-49 points)
- Replace the ground beef with 2 pounds of my Savory Ground Turkey, page 30 *(-30 points)*
- Replace pork sausage with "Italian Sausage" from page 28. *(-17 point)*
- Reduced sugar ketchup instead of regular *(-2 points)*

Sauce: (-12 points)
- Replace regular Ketchup with Reduced Sugar Ketchup. (-5 points)
- Replace Brown Sugar with 3 Tbsp. Sugar Free Maple Syrup (-7 points)

FOUNDATIONS

Recipes for miscellaneous food items used as the building blocks for other meals

What are Foundation Recipes, and why do they need a section? To me, any recipe that is used as the base, or, dare I say... Foundation for a dish, needs special mention. For example, all of the recipes in my upcoming cookbooks will contain one or more of the following foundation recipes.

These are the foundational components of those dishes, such as fresh pasta, ground turkey chorizo, bratwurst and italian sausage, pie crust, yeast pizza dough, masa and more. I thought it would be extremely helpful if I gathered all of my different foundation recipes and compile them all into this one single section, for easy reference.

Use these as the base for your own recipes that you make within the recipe builder. Have a recipe that calls for high point graham cracker crust? Use my low point pie crust instead. Want to hack down the points in a Lasagna recipe? Use my fresh pasta along with my fat free cheese hack. These are the components from which greater dishes are built.

"... blessed are the lowly foundational recipes that act as a base for more fancy dishes, for they shall bless thine tastebuds ..."
- The Book of Freestyle 10:24-25

Foundation Recipes

IMPORTANT NOTE:

All recipes in this book were developed over the course of 15 months. They have all been designed and optimized, by me, for use with the "Freestyle" program, currently the Blue program. Know that WW periodically adjusts the point values of certain ingredients within their database. As a result, there may be a 1 point difference between what my recipes were when they were developed, versus what their point values are "now". You are all encouraged to enter these recipes into your app, to double check the current accuracy of their listed points at this present date.

Asian

Ground turkey or chicken LOADED with asian flavors

Forget "everybody was Kung Fu fighting", as far as I'm concerned, everybody should be making this mix. I came up with this mix, while trying to make my low point Bahn Mi chicken sliders. Though I used ground chicken breast for this recipe, you can definitely use extra lean ground turkey.

Serving Info:
Seasoned Mix
Servings: 8
Serving Size: 2oz

Points: G B P
1 serving =   1   0   0
2 servings = 2   0   0
3 servings = 3   0   0
4 servings = 5   1   1

Ingredients:

- 1lb Ground Chicken Breast (or xtra lean ground turkey)
- 1 Tbsp Asian "fish sauce"
  It's Pretty much, bottled anchovy water. YUM!
- 1-1/2 tsp ground black pepper
- 1 tsp ground ginger
- 3-4 medium garlic cloves, minced
- 1 tsp sesame oil
- 1 Tbsp soy sauce, reduced sodium
- 1/4 tsp baking soda dissolved in 1/2 tsp water *(TRUST ME!!)*
- 1 tsp lime juice
- 1 Tbsp fat free Greek yogurt
- 1/4 cup green onion, thinly chopped (not the white part)
- 1 Tbsp chicken flavored bouillon (granules)

Directions:

- Combine all ingredients in a mixing bowl, until well combined. Allow to sit for 20 minutes, covered.
- Cook as desired.

Bratwurst

Ground Turkey Bratwurst that doesn't suck!?

Guten Morgen, friends! I originally came up with this seasoning blend for my Bratwurst sliders. It took multiple attempts to finally get the seasoning right. Yes, of course the texture of ground turkey isn't the same as ground pork, but... it tastes great, and cuts hundreds of calories.

Serving Info:
Seasoned Mix
Servings: 8
Serving Size: 2oz

Points: G B P
1 serving =   1   0   0
2 servings = 2   0   0
3 servings = 3   0   0
4 servings = 4   0   0

Ingredients:

- 1 pound extra lean ground turkey
- 1 Tbsp beef flavored granules
  (in the soup aisle, or in the mexican food aisle, like the "Knorr" brand)
- 1/2 tsp ground cumin
- 1 tsp onion powder
- 1 tsp garlic powder
- 1/2 tsp smoked paprika
- 3/4 tsp dried mustard
- 1/2 tsp dried sage (might be in the spices as rubbed sage)
- 1/2 tsp dried marjoram
- 1/2 tsp black pepper
- 1/4 tsp baking soda dissolved in 1/2 tsp water *(TRUST ME!!)*
- 3/4 tsp nutmeg
- 1/2 tsp salt
- 3/4 tsp caraway seed
- 1 tsp worcestershire sauce
- 1/2 cup diced onion (*OPTIONAL*, for bulk, if desired)

Directions:

- Combine all ingredients in a mixing bowl, until well combined. Allow to sit for 20 minutes, covered.
- Cook as desired.

Breakfast Sausage

Low Point, Low Calorie Breakfast Sausage

Chorizo

Low calorie, virtually fat free, delicious Chorizo

There are a lot of different low point breakfast sausage recipes out there that call for ground turkey.... this is mine. Mine's a little more on the maple-side of things, because I like that kind of sausage. In this recipe, the sugar free pancake syrup is completely optional. You can replace it with some maple extract from the baking aisle, if you can't have artificial sweeteners. Also, I HIGHLY recommend using the cayenne pepper. Even if you only use a tiny little 1/8 tsp of it, it makes a huge difference.

Serving Info:
Seasoned Mix
Servings: 8
Serving Size: 2oz

Points:
	G	B	P
1 serving =	1	0	0
2 servings =	2	0	0
3 servings =	3	0	0
4 servings =	4	0	0

Ingredients:
- 1 lb extra lean ground turkey
- 1/2 tsp salt
- 1/2 tsp fresh ground pepper
- 1/2 tsp dried sage
- 1 tsp dried thyme
- 1 tsp fennel seed (ground fennel seed is best)
- 1 tsp onion powder
- 1/2 tsp dried marjoram
- 2 tsp 0 point sweetener of choice**
- 1/4 tsp molasses**
- 2 tsp beef flavored granules (like Knorr brand)
- 1/4 tsp baking soda dissolved in 1/2 tsp water *(TRUST ME!!)*
- 1/2 tsp smoked paprika
- 1 Tbsp sugar free pancake syrup
- 1/8-1/4 tsp cayenne pepper to taste
- 1/4 tsp liquid smoke, hickory (OPTIONAL)

Directions:
- Combine all ingredients in a mixing bowl, until well combined. Allow to sit for 20 minutes, covered.
- Cook as desired.

Note:
- Feel free to replace the 0 point sweetener and molasses with 2 tsp of 0 point brown sugar substitute.

Traditional Chorizo is a heavily seasoned, extremely fatty and greasy mixture of ground pork that's loaded with "Pimenton", a type of smoked paprika. If you go to a mexican restaurant and order Chorizo, you'll usually need a good pair of wading pants to get through all of the grease on your plate. My version is really good, has a lot of the traditional flavor, but cuts out 99% of the fat, while still retaining moisture. Mine is ultra low in points, so feel free to add more smoked paprika if you want, but adjust your points accordingly, as always.

Serving Info:
YIELDS: 4 cups
Servings: 8
Serving Size: 2oz

Points:
	G	B	P
1 serving =	1	0	0
2 servings =	2	0	0
3 servings =	3	0	0
4 servings =	5	1	1

Ingredients:
- 1 lb extra lean ground turkey
- 3 tsp minced garlic (3 med. cloves)
- 1 Tbsp chili powder
- 2 tsp paprika
- 1/2 tsp smoked paprika
- 3/4 tsp salt
- 1/2 tsp pepper
- 1 tsp dried oregano
- 1/4 or 1/2 tsp cayenne pepper or chipotle powder *(to taste)*
- 1/2 tsp ground cumin
- 1/2 tsp ground coriander
- 1/4 tsp ground cinnamon
- 1/4 tsp baking soda dissolved in 1/2 tsp water *(TRUST ME!!)*
- 1 Tbsp beef flavored granules (like Knorr brand)
- 2 Tbsp apple cider vinegar

Directions:
- Combine all ingredients in a mixing bowl, until well combined. Allow to sit for 20 minutes, covered.
- Cook as desired.

Cuban Picadillo

Delicious latin flavors with lime and cinnamon

This is tied with Kafta for the most flavorful of all of these mixes. It tastes so insanely good. It has strong notes of typical latin flavors, like cumin and oregano... but then you get slapped with little pops of olive, lime and even the exotic hint of cinnamon. It sounds so weird, but it tastes SO GOOD!

Serving Info:
Seasoned Mix
Servings: 12
Serving Size: 2oz

Points:

	G	B	P
1 serving =	1	0	0
2 servings =	2	0	0
3 servings =	3	1	1
4 servings =	3	1	1

Ingredients:

- 1lb extra lean ground turkey
- 3 tsp beef flavored granules (bouillon)
- 1/2 tsp onion powder
- 1/2 tsp garlic powder
- 1-1/2 tsp worcestershire sauce
- 1-1/2 tsp ground cumin
- 1/2 tsp dried oregano
- 1/4 tsp baking soda dissolved in 1/2 tsp water *(TRUST ME!!)*
- 1/2 tsp salt
- 1/4 tsp pepper
- 6 green olives, stuffed with pimientos, chopped
  (don't get the HUGE olives, you want 6 for 1 point)
- 1 small red bell pepper, finely diced (around 1/2 cup)
- 1 small green bell pepper, finely diced (around 1/2 cup)
- 1 Tbsp raisins, chopped
- 2 medium garlic cloves, minced
- 1/4 tsp ground cinnamon
- 1 Tbsp lime juice
- 1/4 cup fresh chopped cilantro

Directions:

- Mix everything together in a large mixing bowl, until well combined. Allow to sit for 20 minutes, covered. Cook until browned.

Italian Sausage

Awesome, 0 point Italian Sausage substitute

When I was trying to lose my weight, when I dove into WW, one thing that I REALLY wanted was Italian sausage, but let's face it... I'm the Ebenezer Scrooge of Points, so I couldn't make myself use my points on pork sausage. I tried tons of different versions of this recipe, before finally coming up with this baby.

Serving Info:
Seasoned Mix
Servings: 8
Serving Size: 2oz

Points:

	G	B	P
1 serving =	1	0	0
2 servings =	2	0	0
3 servings =	3	0	0
4 servings =	4	0	0

Ingredients:

- 1 lb extra lean ground turkey
- 1 tsp ground fennel seed *(you can use whole seed, but I prefer ground)*
- 1 tsp garlic powder
- 1 tsp onion powder
- 1 tsp dried italian seasoning
- 1/2 tsp dried basil
- 1 Tbsp dried parsley
- 1/4 tsp baking soda dissolved in 1/2 tsp water *(TRUST ME!!)*
- 1/2 tsp salt
- 1/4 tsp fresh ground pepper
- 3/4 tsp paprika
- 2 Tbsp red wine vinegar
- 1 Tbsp beef or chicken granules (bouillon)
- red pepper flakes to taste (OPTIONAL)

Directions:

- Combine all ingredients in a mixing bowl, until well combined. Allow to sit for 20 minutes, covered.
- Cook as desired.

Jerk Seasoning

A spicy and savory Caribbean spice blend

No, you don't need to be a meanie-head to make this. "Jerk" is a traditional Jamaican seasoning, normally used on chicken. It typically calls for chopped scotch bonnet peppers, which are hotter than satan's kidney stones. I decided to tone it down a little, by using Habanero peppers, which are easier to find in grocery stores. This mix has it all. Exotic spices, a good deal of heat, a little sweet, and a little acidity from lime juice and zest.

Serving Info:
Seasoned Mix
Servings: 8
Serving Size: 2oz

Points: G B P
	G	B	P
1 serving =	1	0	0
2 servings =	2	0	0
3 servings =	3	0	0
4 servings =	5	1	1

Ingredients:
- 1lb extra lean ground turkey
- 1 medium garlic clove, finely chopped
- 1-1/2 tsp fresh ginger, finely chopped
- 3 Tbsp green onion, thinly sliced
- 2 medium cloves garlic, minced
- 2 tsp lime juice
- 1 tsp lime zest, minced
- 2 tsp soy sauce, reduced sodium
- 1/4 tsp baking soda dissolved in 1/2 tsp water **(TRUST ME!!)**
- 1 tsp fresh thyme, finely chopped
- 2 tsp brown sugar
- 1/2 tsp ground allspice
- 1/4 tsp ground cinnamon
- 1/4 tsp black pepper
- 1/4 tsp nutmeg
- 1/2 tsp cayenne pepper
- 2 habanero peppers, deseeded, finely diced **(use gloves!!)**
- 2 tsp chicken or beef flavored bouillon

Directions:
- Combine all ingredients in a mixing bowl, until well combined. Allow to rest for a minimum of 20 minutes.
- Cook as desired.

Lebanese Kafta

This baby's like taking a trip to a Kabob House

Kafta is Lebanese a ground meat mixture, usually ground beef or lamb, mixed with a ton of fresh parsley, onion, and seasonings. This is a hybrid of my father's traditional recipe and my own "savory ground turkey". It has a deep, savory, beefy flavor and you won't believe that this is ground turkey.

Serving Info:
Seasoned Mix
Servings: 10
Serving Size: 2oz

Points: G B P
	G	B	P
1 serving =	1	0	0
2 servings =	2	0	0
3 servings =	2	0	0
4 servings =	3	0	0

Ingredients:
- 1lb extra lean ground turkey
- 1 Tbsp beef flavored bouillon
- 1 tsp onion powder
- 1 tsp garlic powder
- 1/2 tsp smoked paprika
- 1/2 tsp ground cumin
- 2 tsp worcestershire sauce
- 1/4 tsp salt
- 1/4 tsp black pepper
- 3/4 tsp ground allspice
- 3/4 tsp ground cinnamon
- 1/4 tsp baking soda dissolved in 1/2 tsp water **(TRUST ME!!)**
- 1/2 cup fresh parsley, finely chopped, loosely packed
- 3/4 cup onion, finely diced/chopped
- 3-4 garlic medium cloves garlic, minced

Directions:
- Combine all ingredients in a mixing bowl, until well combined. Allow to rest for a minimum of 20 minutes.
- Cook as desired.

Linguica

A smoky and spicy Portuguese sausage mix

Savory Mix

A versatile mix that gives a deep, beefy flavor

Linguica is a super fatty, smoked and very spicy Portuguese sausage. My version is a low fat, calorie and point seasoning blend that gets its smokiness from smoked paprika and a touch of liquid smoke. The heat comes from black pepper and red pepper flakes, which you can adjust to your own tastes. Still... this is SUPPOSED to be a bit spicy.

Serving Info:

Seasoned Mix
Servings: 8
Serving Size: 2oz

Points:

	G	B	P
1 serving =	1	0	0
2 servings =	2	0	0
3 servings =	3	0	0
4 servings =	4	1	1

Ingredients:

- 1lb extra lean ground turkey
- 1 Tbsp chicken (or beef) flavored granules (bouillon)
- 1-3/4 tsp salt
- 3/4 tsp black pepper
- 1/8 to 1/2 tsp red pepper flakes *(TO TASTE)*
- 1/4 tsp baking soda dissolved in 1/2 tsp water *(TRUST ME!!)*
- 1 tsp liquid smoke (I used Hickory flavored)
- 2 tsp smoked paprika
- 1 tsp paprika
- 3/4 tsp dried oregano
- 1 Tbsp red wine vinegar
- 1 tsp 0 point sugar substitute of choice (swerve, splenda, stevia, monkfruit, etc)

Directions:

- Combine all ingredients in a mixing bowl, until well combined. Allow to rest for a minimum of 20 minutes.
- Cook as desired.

I use this recipe whenever I need a standard, beefy flavor for a dish. What's the one complaint that you hear about ground turkey from EVERYONE? "It tastes bland...It's dry... It has no flavor". Well, of course it doesn't, so OPEN YOUR SPICE CABINET AND FIX THAT! A lot of thought went into this mix. Think that ground turkey has no flavor? Add beef bouillon, smoked paprika, worcestershire and a touch of cumin. Now you have ground turkey that's saturated with beefy, smoky, earthy flavors.

Serving Info:

Seasoned Mix
Servings: 8
Serving Size: 2oz

Points:

	G	B	P
1 serving =	1	0	0
2 servings =	2	0	0
3 servings =	3	0	0
4 servings =	4	0	0

Ingredients:

- 1lb extra lean ground turkey
- 3 tsp beef flavored granules
- 1 tsp onion powder
- 1 tsp garlic powder
- 1/2 tsp smoked paprika
- 1/2 tsp ground cumin
- 1/4 tsp baking soda dissolved in 1/2 tsp water *(TRUST ME!!)*
- 1 tsp low sodium soy sauce
- 2 tsp worcestershire sauce
- 1/4 tsp black pepper
- 1/4 tsp salt

Directions:

- Combine all ingredients in a mixing bowl, until well combined. Allow to rest for a minimum of 20 minutes.
- Cook as desired.

Note:

- This recipe works great as a stand in for ground beef for most recipes, such as burgers, shepherd's pie, sloppy joes, meatloaf and much more.

Things You'll Need:

Chicken & Beef Flavored Granules

Add Instant Deep Flavor
Wish that ground turkey tasted more like beef or chicken? IT CAN! There are many different brands of bouillon at your local grocery store, but they are not all created equal. Some are lower or higher in points, sodium and calories than others. Most Walmarts carry the Knorr brand, which I use in anything that has ground turkey. While most brands will turn to 1 point at 2 or 3 teaspoons, Knorr stays at 0 points until you use 3-1/2 teaspoons. At the majority of supermarkets, you most likely won't find it in the soup aisle, which is where you'd THINK to find it. 99% of the time it'll be in the aisle with the Mexican or Latin foods, even at Walmart. Scan any brand of granulated bouillon that you find, to make sure you get a brand that stays at 0 points for 1 Tablespoon. If you can't find one, get what you can, but adjust how much you use, to stay 0 points. <u>LEAVE OUT the granules if using Beef.</u>

Cooking Sprays (say whaaaaaa?)

Stop Being So Tacky!
I used to have everyone put a dollop of Greek yogurt into all of my ground meat mixtures to help add moisture. Dry ground turkey isn't an issue anymore, ever since we started adding that tiny bit of dissolved baking soda into the recipes. It makes the meat incredibly juicy and alters the texture of the final product. However... there is one issue that you can have sometimes, namely, that after allowing the meat to rest for 20 minutes, it can become very sticky/tacky. It's frustrating, because it's very difficult to handle if you're trying to form the meat into patties or meatballs. The solution is simple, 0 point cooking sprays.

Most all cooking sprays will allow you to use a certain amount for 0 points, depending on the brand. If the meat is too tacky, hit it with a quick burst of cooking spray, then flip the raw meat over and lightly spray the other side. You should then be able to pick it up and form the meat, no problem.

Meatballs

Make ANY of these mixes into meatballs
With a 1lb batch of the meat mixes, use a measuring spoon to scoop out 1 Tbsp rounds of meat. When rolled they make perfect snack sized meatballs. You can get around 30 out of 1 pound, or 15 2 Tbsp sized meatballs. I've had good luck baking them at 425 for 15 minutes.

Baking Soda

What'chu talkin 'bout, Willis??
I wish I could explain the science behind it, but this is a legit game changer. I was browsing an old French cooking site one night, and came upon a technique for making ground meat awesome. For every 1lb of ground meat, mix in 1/4 tsp of baking soda dissolved with 1/2 tsp of water, then allow the meat to rest for 30 minutes before cooking. It completely changes the texture of the meat. It retains a TON of it's own moisture. You know how when you normally cook ground turkey, it's swimming in a pool of it's own liquids? Who wants grey meat! Doing this locks in so much liquid, that the meat ends up more juicy AND it browns in the pan sooooo much better. It's a flippin' Vatican-worthy miracle, imho. Ground turkey ends up having a texture closer to cooked ground pork, which makes these seasonings REALLY sing. Give it a try, you won't regret it. **NOTE: Though this works amazing with ground turkey, I would not recommend it with ground chicken. The baking soda makes chicken have a slightly tough exterior, though it gives ground turkey a great texture and mouth feel.**

Cuban Picadillo Turkey Meatballs

2 Ingredient Dough

The simple yet versatile dough recipe that keeps us sane

Points:

	G	B	P
1 cup ball =	14	12	12
1/4 balls =	4	3	3
1/8 ball =	2	2	2

If you've been in-program for any length of time you KNOW how much you missed your bread when you first started. I'm including this in the book because there are a lot of new people who still view 2 ingredient dough as a mystery and ask in Connect "How do you make it? What's in it?" For you new folks, this dough is so incredibly versatile, it truly is the kitchen chameleon. I use this stuff for everything. breakfast pizzas, bagels, steamed for Asian inspired dumplings, thrown it into a hearty low point chicken and dumplings, strombolis, biscuits, impromptu projectiles, the list goes on and on.

Ingredients:

- 1 cup Self Rising flour
- 3/4 cup Fat Free Greek Yogurt
- additional water IF NEEDED

Directions:

1. Combine the Flour and Yogurt in a mixing bowl until well combined and formed into a ball.
2. Remove from bowl and place on cutting board dusted with flour.
3. Basic cooking method:
   Bake at 375 for 18-20 min.

Various Applications:

- Quarter the dough as pictured below, and use the 4 separate 3sp sections for a variety of uses such as 3sp Bagels, Biscuits, flattened into rounds to make 4 small personal sized pizzas, and much more.
- Cut the dough into 1/8th's instead of 1/4's to make small 2-3sp dough balls for use as bread knots, small dessert bread bites and appetizers.
- Roll the dough out into long ropes and slice it into small dumplings for use in low point chicken and dumplings.
- Steam the dough to make asian buns.

- If you roll out the dough ball into 1 large round pizza dough rather than sectioning it into quarters, you can use it to make a regular sized medium pizza or a larger sized thin crust pizza.
- Roll out the dough and use it to make calzones and strombolis.
- If you're on the **PURPLE** plan, replace some of the Greek with mashed potato, and add extra baking powder for soft potato bread.
- Another version is "*3 ingredient dough*". Use 2 cups self rising flour, 1 cup yogurt and 2 eggs. Mix together and portion just like normal. It's more airy and fluffy.

** *Cook temp & time vary depending on application*

(1) 1 cup portion

(4) 1/4 cup portions

(8) 1/8 cup portions

Pizza Dough

If you are looking for a fast, reliable and easy way to make a basic pizza crust that's easy to portion for different amounts of Points, then 2 ingredient dough is a godsend. You can use a 1 cup dough ball to flatten/stretch into a good medium sized thin crust pizza that will only cost 12 points all together in crust. For a comparison, the ready-made pizza dough available at major grocery store chain "*Jrader Toes*" ***cough*** is over 35 points.

You can also make 4 personal sized pizzas out of the 1 cup dough ball by cutting it into equal 1/4's, each one being 3 Points. When rolled out they are each the size of a personal sized pizza. Or if you want a Small sized pizza, simply cut the dough ball in 1/2 for 2 small pizzas that are 6 points for each crust. Though cook times vary depending on each person's preference, typically everyone bakes their 2 ingredient pizzas at 425 degrees for between 20-25 minutes, depending on how they like their crust.

Bagels, Biscuits, and Preztels

For those of us that aren't nutcase carb-cutters like some of the trend "diets" turn you in to, using 2 ingredient dough to make bagels, biscuits and pretzels is a game changer in our weight loss journey. For regular sized bagels, biscuits, and pretzels you should quarter the 1 cup dough ball, making (4) 3 point sections. For bagels, roll each section into a thick rope and then twist it into a round bagel shape. Pretzels are prepared in the same way except the rope of dough is twisted into a pretzel shape. You can then spray each piece with butter flavored cooking spray, sprinkled it with your desired seasonings and bake. Typical baking directions for bagels is: 350 degrees for 20 minutes, then turn up the heat to 450 degrees for a final 2-3 minute to brown the top a little more. For REAL, browned and chewy bagels, boil a pot of water with 1/4 cup of baking soda in it. When your raw dough is shaped into rounds, boil them for 30 seconds on each side. Take the boiled bagels out of the baking soda bath, then bake them at 425 until dark brown, about 13-15 minutes. They are 10x more awesome that way.

Snack Sized Bites

Other than pizzas and big delicious bagel sized fluffy goodness, there are even more ways to utilize this dough. Rather than sectioning it into (4) 3 point sections, you can section the 1 cup dough ball into 8 separate smaller point sections. 1 piece is 2 points, 2 pieces is 3 points and each additional section scales up accordingly (+1 point, +2 points, +1 point).

You can use these smaller sections for a ton of different small bites and appetizer ideas such as bite sized pretzel nuggets, rolling the rounds in your sweetener of choice and cinnamon, form the sections into small flat tortilla-like rounds with a filling in the center and then roll them up into a stuffed bread ball with any number of fillings.. the options are endless. Cooking temperatures and bake times vary depending on what type of snack sized appetizer you are trying to make. A quick search online or in Connect will find tons of recipe ideas.

Empanadas/Stuffed Pockets

2 ingredient dough is also a fantastic vehicle to make savory stuffed breads and pastries. Using the same exact principles as all of the other applications, you can simply fold your preferred filling of choice inside two layers of the dough to make sweet or savory stuffed empanadas, calzones, stromboli, baked panini sandwiches, baked breakfast pockets filled with scrambled eggs, cheese, veggies... you are only bound by the limits of your culinary imagination.

You can find hundreds of delicious recipes and ideas on Connect or any number of websites such as pinterest, emilybites and skinnytaste.

@mappleby777

@mugglemama2017

@julieo145

@mappleby777

Low Point Breading 1.0

Sometimes You Have To Get Creative To Game The System

Guilt Free Breading

I'll be the first to admit that I went a little crazy-overboard during my weight loss phase of my journey. I went nearly half a year without eating anything that was breaded because of how point conscious/paranoid I was. Then one day after reaching goal, a thought occured to me. In the recipe builder I noticed that if I added 2tsp of all purpose flour to a recipe it was 1 point, but if I added 2 different types of flour with 1-1/2tsp of EACH, that it was still 0 points even though I now had 3tsp of flour. So that made me go into the builder to see how I could outsmart it with amounts of different crumbs. This is the result.

Ingredients:

- 2 egg whites
- 1 Tbsp Water
- 1 Tbsp Fat Free Plain Yogurt (or Greek)
- 1 tsp Dijon Mustard (optional)
- 1/2 cups Instant Mashed Potato Flakes
- 2 tsp Panko Bread Crumbs
- 3 Tbsp Plain Bread Crumbs
- Additional Herbs & Seasonings to Taste
- Cooking Spray

Directions:

1 Whisk together the egg whites, water, yogurt, & mustard (if using), in a wide bowl or dish.
2 In a separate container, mix together the flakes, bread crumbs, desired herbs and seasonings.
3 Pat your prepared meat dry with paper towels if necessary to ensure that they are dry.
4 Lightly dredge your meat cutlets, 1 at a time, through the egg-wash, lifting it up and allowing excess eggwash to run back into the bowl.
5 Place the meat into the dish with your breading and lightly coat both sides.
6 Place the breaded meat on a dish and liberally coat with cooking spray on both sides.
7 Cook the breaded meat according to your recipes directions.

Yields:

Makes enough breading to coat 4 medium sized chicken breasts

	G	B	P
Points: 1 serving =	1	1	1
2 servings =	3	3	3
3 servings =	4	4	4

COOKING TIP:

If baking, for best results bake the breaded cutlets on a wire rack on top of your baking pan to allow for heat to circulate around all sides of the chicken. It will keep the bottom of the meat raised off of the surface so that it gets crispy on both sides.

Low Point Breading 2.0

Snap Crackle Pop, Rice Breadiiiiiiing

That breading recipe, over yonder, that says 1.0... I put that together around a year and a half ago, this my upgrade. I came up with this one not too long ago, back when *@andmatsmom*, mentioned to me how people used to make pie crust with crushed rice krispies because of the points. That got me thinking, "I wonder if you could use it for breading?" Aaaand here we are.

Breading:
- 1-1/4 cup crispy rice cereal (like rice krispies). Place it in a ziplock bag and crush it. You'll end up with around 2/3 cup.
- 1-1/2 tsp plain breadcrumbs
- 2 tsp panko breadcrumbs
- 1/4 tsp salt
- 1/4 tsp black pepper
- 1/4 tsp garlic powder
- 1/4 tsp onion powder
- 1/2 tsp italian seasoning

Egg Wash:
- 2 large eggs
- 1-1/2 tsp self rising flour
- 1-1/2 tsp cornstarch
- 1 tsp dijon mustard
- 1/2 tsp water

Directions:

1. Prepare the egg wash. Whisk together the 2 eggs, set aside.
2. In a small dish, stir together the flour, cornstarch, dijon mustard and water into a smooth, thick paste. Whisk into the beaten eggs. It will slightly thicken the egg wash.
3. In a large ziplock bag, crush the rice krispie cereal until it has the same texture as plain breadcrumbs. Pour into a bowl.
4. Add the panko, regular breadcrumbs, salt, pepper, garlic powder, onion powder and italian seasoning (optional). Stir to mix.
5. Now, it's pretty self explanatory. Dip things in the egg, let the excess run off into the bowl. Then lightly coat with the breading.
6. Spray the breaded items with cooking spray, on a foil lined pan.
7. Once breaded, I typically use this to bake things at 425 degrees for around 15 minutes, or until browned.

Servings Info.:

Yield: about 3/4 cup breading
Servings: Dependent upon how you use it. It can bread 4 large chicken breasts, or a sheet pan of onion rings.

Points:		G	B	P
	1 serving =	2	1	1
	2 servings =	4	2	2
	3 servings =	6	3	3

Note:

- If you are on the GREEN plan, use 2 egg whites instead of regular eggs. It will then have the exact same points per serving as the BLUE and PURPLE plans.
- This breading is used in a few of the appetizers later in this book.
- This versatile breading works great on anything. Zucchini, banana bites, chicken strips, clams...

"Cream Cheese"

Turning Greek Yogurt into a fat free Cream Cheese Substitute

DIY Fat Free "Cream Cheese" Substitute

First off, I need to give credit where it's due and thank "*@mickeydoyle5*" from Connect for tipping me off to this ingredient hack that I had never heard of before. Once I heard about it I HAD to try it considering how much fat free cream cheese I go through with my cupcakes. THIS STUFF IS AWESOME!!! Make sure that you use a Greek Yogurt with a very mild "tang" to it, as a lot of Greek Yogurts have a very sharp taste that sucks the life & happiness out of desserts normally. I used Chobani Fat Free Greek Yogurt, though my ABSOLUTE FAVORITE is FAGE 0%. Fage is a little pricier but it has the least amount of yogurt tang of all the major brands. It is an almost perfect match to a slightly softened cream cheese with juuuust a tiny bit of bite to it. I personally think that it works as a wonderful sub for cream cheese in dips, spreads and in appetizers. Some folks have been using this in cheesecake recipes with success, which inspired me to start using it in place of cream cheese for my frostings.

Yields: 6 cups

Servings: The servings is completely dependent on the application for which you plan to use the strained yogurt. Below, I will post the TOTAL POINTS for the entire container's worth of yogurt. Use as much or as little as your recipe requires.

Ⓖ Ⓑ Ⓟ

Total Points: 17 0 0

*This is the amount of points for the **ENTIRE** 35oz of Greek yogurt. If you are on the Green plan, your points per serving will be dependent on your recipe*

What You'll Need:

- 35oz FAGE (or other mild) Fat Free Greek Yogurt
- Cheese Cloth (or paper coffee filters)
- Strainer
- Large Bowl
- Plastic Wrap

Directions:

1 Attach or set a plastic or metal strainer onto a large bowl or pot in such a way that the strainer will not come in contact with any liquid that drips to the bottom.
2 Line the bowl of the strainer with 6-8 layers of cheesecloth or paper coffee liners (much cheaper).
3 Pour all of the Greek Yogurt onto the cheesecloth.
4 Cover it all with plastic wrap and set in the refrigerator for at least 24 hours (mine was fine at 24).
5 Store in an air tight container for up to 1 week and use in place of regular cream cheese.

Note:

- If you are unable to get cheese cloth, you can line your strainer with a few layers of paper coffee filters.

0 point creamy awesomeness

How To Make It Melt

There has always been one constant truth in the Universe, that Fat Free Cheese can't melt. Actually it can, it's just always done a really bad job of melting. (It sucks at it, actually.)

One afternoon while cooking I accidentally dropped some fat free cheese on the kitchen counter and it landed up against a little dab of yogurt. I was feeling lazy and decided to clean it up later. However when I came back, the two had kind of melded together, which gave me the idea to try this.

By mixing ANY amount of fat free shredded cheese with roughly 1/2 as much fat free plain or greek yogurt, then using it as a spread, you can "cheese" a pizza, lasagna, casserole, any dish you want, for virtually no points compared to regular cheese. It sounds so wrong... but it's so right. Once exposed to high heat, the yogurt and cheese both melt together..

Fat Free Cheese Hack

How To Make Fat Free Cheeses Melt Like Regular Cheese

Ingredients:

- Any amount of Fat Free Shredded Cheese
- Roughly 1/2 to 3/4 as much Fat Free Plain or Greek Yogurt

Directions:

1 Take any amount of Fat Free Shredded Cheese *(or low fat cheese if you would like to make that more melty as well)* and mix it in a mixing bowl with the yogurt until well combined into a thick ricotta-like sticky mixture.
2 Spread or dollop the cheese onto the surface of the dish you would like it to melt on. Cook in the same manner that you would regular cheese. (IE: Baked into a casserole, on top of Chicken Parmesan, etc)

COOKING TIPS:

- A huge benefit of this versus just rinsing off the cheese to help it melt is that the yogurt adds volume to the cheese, stretching it further in your recipe. Add 1 cup of yogurt to 2 cups of cheese. You now have 3 cups of cheese spread for the points of 2 cups.
- The "Point" value for this technique is based entirely upon how much fat free cheese you decide to use. The Yogurt has 0 points, so all that you are accounting for when building your recipe to determine points-per-serving is the cheese.

Points & Servings:

The points and number of servings is completely dependent upon how much of the cheese you use and how you will be using it. You will need to figure out the points for yourself, based upon your needs.

Masa & Tortillas

Latin American cuisine would be nowhere without Masa, a dough made from very finely ground corn, which is used to make Tortillas, Tamales, Gorditas, Sopes... it is everything in Latin cooking. Think of it like the all purpose flour that you're used to using for biscuits, rolls, pizza dough, and other common baked goods. The flour required to make Masa is in most all grocery stores, typically found in either the Latin/Ethnic section or by where the Cornmeal is sold, sometimes labeled as "Maseca, Instant Tamale Mix." Note, this is NOT a traditional recipe, this is my version. I like my tortillas a little softer, so I add yogurt in place of lard. This makes the masa softer and also helps the texture should you choose to make tamales by adding the additional baking powder.

Ingredients:

- 2 cups Masa Harina, Maseca, or other brand Instant Corn Masa (corn flour NOT cornmeal!!)
- 1-1/4 cup Water
- 1/2 cup Fat Free Plain or Greek Yogurt
- 1/2 tsp salt
- Additional water if needed for mixing
  *** *(add 2tsp baking powder if being used to make Tamales)*
  *** *(use chicken broth instead of water, if making Tamales)*

Directions:

1. In a large mixing bowl, combine the corn flour, 1-1/4 cups water, yogurt, and salt. Mix thoroughly until you form a semi-firm dough ball. If dough appears dry while mixing, add additional water as needed.

SERVING SIZE & POINTS:

- The servings & points vary, depending on how much you use. For tortillas I use 1/8 portions, for tamales I use 1/4 portions. The points listed below are for 1/8 sections, which make a good sized tortilla, using a tortilla press.

Points:		G	B	P
1 serving =		2	2	2
2 servings =		3	3	3
3 servings =		5	5	5

2. Remove dough to a cutting board, and cut into 2 equal sized 1 cup dough balls. Then portion each 1 cup dough ball into 1/4's and then into 1/8's sized portions.

3. Roll each one of the 16 small dough sections into a circular ball. Then, on a flat surface, use your palm and fingers to press the dough balls into tortilla sized rounds.

4. For perfectly uniform tortillas, you can use a traditional tortilla press to form them. They are fairly inexpensive and can be purchased at most ethnic grocery stores, walmarts, or online, for around $10.-15. Get a metal one.

5. To cook the tortillas, heat a skillet, griddle, or large pan on medium-high heat. Cook each tortilla for around 45 seconds on each side.

6. Keep tortillas warm by placing them in a covered container, or place them on a plate covered with a dish cloth. Tortillas are best served warm... unlike revenge.

A FEW DIFFERENT USES:

A) Sopes - Traditionally, the base is made from a circle of fried masa with sides pinched up to resemble a shallow cup. However for WW purposes you should spray it with cooking spray and then bake it. This can then be topped with any number of toppings. Bake the shells at 350 degrees for 10-15 minutes.

B) Tamales - If you are a WW member, you can view a video in Connect where I show how to make 3 point Tamales. Search for #dhallaktamales and scroll down to my DIY Tamale video.

C) Arepas - Arepas are awesome. For best results use a 3 point 1/4 cup section of the Masa dough, form it into a 1/2" thick tortilla round. For the non-fried WW version, cook it on a hot griddle or pan for 45 seconds on each side, and then remove it from the heat and slice it ALMOST completely in half down its length like a big pocket. Stuff it with fillings of your choice, then return it to heat.

D) If you need me to explain what a Taco is... put down this book. Put it down. No really, put it down. No food for you.

COOKING TIP:

- You can easily HALF this recipe if you don't want to make a big batch.
- If you plan to make Tamales OR Arepas, make sure to add 1 tsp of baking powder to each cup of flour that you use to help them fluff up a little bit.
- If you would like to NOT use the yogurt in this recipe due to dairy allergies, you can replace it with an equal amount of silken tofu.
- If you would like an even MORE chewie tortilla, you can substitute 1/4 cup of the corn flour with 1/4 cup of all purpose flour. I personally love the texture that way... but I'm a full-on Gringo.
- If you buy a tortilla press, I would recommend a metal one. They are a few dollars more, but they are more durable. I've broken 2 plastic ones from the hinges breaking with too much pressure.
- Instead of a tortilla press you can put one of the balls of masa between 2 layers of plastic wrap and press down with a pot.
- For more savory tortillas add 1/2 tsp garlic and onion powder to the flour.

Pasta Basics

Make Your Own Low Point, Low Calorie Pasta

Two of the biggest heartaches you hear in Connect are how much people miss their pastas and how many points they blow on pasta dishes. I used to think the same way. I went MONTHS without having pasta because I didn't want to spend the points. Then I started looking into it and realized that making your own pasta is lower in points, calories and carbs, is tastier than store bought dried pasta and you get A LOT more pasta for the points.

Ingredients:

- 2 cups of all purpose flour (or your flour of choice)
- 3 large eggs
- 1/2 tsp salt (optional)
- 2 Tbsp water
- 5 sprays, olive oil cooking spray
- additional water for mixing, as needed, 1 tsp at a time
  ** up to 1 additional Tbsp of flour, for dusting

Directions:

1. In a large mixing bowl or stand mixer, combine the flour, eggs, salt, olive oil cooking spray and 2 Tbsp of water to form a dough ball. The mixture will be dry, so add water as needed to help the dough come together. We aren't adding all of the water all at once because we want to cut down on how much flour we have to use for dusting later on. Wet dough = bad.

2. Remove dough to a cutting board, and cut into 2 equal sized 1 cup dough balls. I typically wrap and keep 1 of them in the freezer so that I can thaw it out and have ready-made pasta dough at a later time. For this recipe, we will assume that you are doing the same.

Yields: (8) 1/4 cup dough balls

Points:

	G	B	P
1 serving =	4	3	3
2 servings =	8	7	7
3 servings =	12	10	10

Use Whole Wheat flour, on the **PURPLE PLAN** and this becomes 0 point whole wheat pasta.

3. Take 1 of your 1 cup pasta dough balls, and cut it into (4) 1/4 cup portions, just like when you section 2 ingredient dough. Next, roll each one of the 1/4 cup sections into 4 small dough balls.

4. The dough balls vary in points. The first 1/4 cup balls is 3 points, the 2nd ball is 7, the 3rd is 10 and the 4th ball is 13. If you want slightly more pasta, roll the 1 cup ball into a log, then cut it into 3 equal 1/3 cup servings, rather than (4) 1/4 cup servings. Adjust your points accordingly.

5. Use your hand and a rolling pin to flatten one of the 1/4 cup pasta balls into a roughly rectangular flat shape. *(Read Notes for instructions for dusting the dough)***

6. You are trying to shape your flattened dough balls to fit length-wise across most of the pasta makers guide-track.

7. With the pasta-width adjustment at its widest setting, run the pasta through the sheet rollers 3-4 times, then adjust the knob on the machine to make the rollers 1 step closer together.

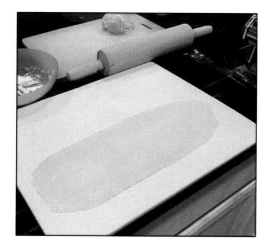

8. After every 3-4 passes through the rollers, continue to make the pasta sheet thinner and thinner, stopping after the 2nd from the thinnest setting.

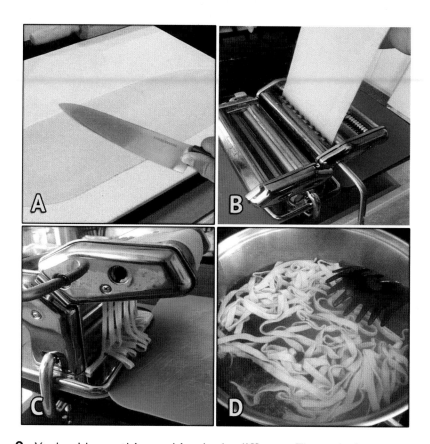

9. Yeah... I know this machine looks different. These 4 pics were taken today, 7 months later, with a new pasta maker 👻 **(A)** Use a knife to cut your pasta sheet in half, then use a few taps of the remaining flour in your wire strainer, to lightly dust the pasta sheet on both sides. **(B)** Move hand crank to the hole for the linguini cutter. Hold one of the pasta sheet halves over the unit, positioning the bottom of the sheet against the cutting blades. **(C)** Turn the hand crank, while lowering the pasta sheet into the blades. **(D)** As soon as the noodles are cut, drop them into a pot of boiling water. Use a utensil to stir and separate them. Boil for 2 minutes then remove from water and strain. Repeat until all of the pasta is rolled out, cut into noodles and boiled. Use immediately by stirring them into a sauce. If you need to save them for later, rinse the noodles off with cool water and store in a ziplock bag in the fridge. Reheat by putting them back into boiling water for a few seconds.

COOKING TIP:

- **DUSTING:** Traditionally, chefs don't "dust" dough with flour, they freakin DUMP fist fulls of flour onto it. For this recipe, take 1-1/2 tsp of flour and put it into a fine mesh wire strainer. When you need to dust your dough with flour, lightly tap the strainer over the dough instead. Also, you can lightly spritz the dough with cooking spray, as seen in my Youtube video for making low point pasta dough and noodles.
- If you are making lasagna I would highly recommend boiling the pasta sheets first then rinsing them off. Boiling them will make them get MUCH bigger, plus it will give them a slightly firmer texture.
- If you do not have a stand mixer to mix your dough you can either mix it by hand in a mixing bowl, or you can actually mix the dough VERY quickly in a food processor. Check out my video in **Youtube** channel, **"The Guilt Free Gourmet"** to find the food processor pasta dough video.
- If you are allergic to gluten, Bob's Red Mill has a great certified Gluten Free, Celiac-friendly, All Purpose Flour, available at most major markets.

Ricotta Gnocchi

Making fresh Ricotta Gnocchi without special equipment

As much as I enjoy making pasta from scratch, most folks in WW don't. Let's face it... it's intimidating. I needed to figure out a way to show people how easy it could be to make their own delicious pasta, without needing any special equipment or pasta machines. Well, now all people have to do is make dough, roll it into ropes, cut it into nuggets and boil. Done.

The KEY to these dumplings is that you want to cut them small. They are not meant to be the bulk of a dish. Fortify them with lots of 0 point veggies, meats, and a low point sauce. You want to stretch the 1/4 cup servings as far as you can. They are the star of a dish, not the bulk of it.

Yields:
(2) 1 cup Dough Balls
(8) 1/4 cup servings.
Each 1/4 cup serving yields around 70 small dumplings per 1/4 cup

Points:

	G	B	P
1 serving =	4	4	4
2 servings =	8	7	7
3 servings =	12	11	11

NOTES:
- You can use fat free cottage cheese in place of the ricotta, to take the first serving down to 3 points.
- On the **PURPLE PLAN**, use whole wheat flour to make these, and you're TECHNICALLY making whole wheat pasta. The points would drop to 0 points for 1 serving and up to 5 servings for only 1 point.

Ingredients:

- 2 cups All Purpose Flour *(or your preferred flour)*
- 1 tsp baking powder
- 2 large eggs
- 1/2 cup Fat Free Ricotta Cheese
- 1/2 tsp salt
- olive oil cooking spray
- additional water to mix (around 1/4 cup)

Directions:

1. In a large mixing bowl, combine the flour, baking powder, eggs, ricotta and salt to form a dough ball. Add extra water as necessary to just help the ball come together. The dough should be the texture of semi firm play dough. Not too firm, but still soft.

2. Cut the 2 cup dough ball into 2 equal sized 1 cup dough balls. Wrap one in plastic wrap and store in the freezer for later use if you only want to make a 1 cup batch. Otherwise, prepare both sections.

3. Cut the 1 cup dough ball section into (4) 1/4 cup, then cut those in half into small 1/8 cup sections.

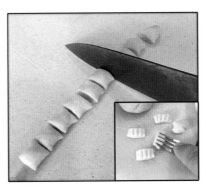

5. Cut each strand into small gnocchi. You should be able to get around 60-70 small gnocchi per 1/4 cup section. Then, lightly press down on each dumpling with a small fork, to give them a gnocchi "look" and make them slightly larger.

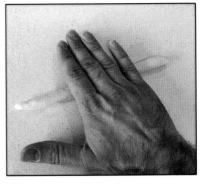

4. Roll each 1/8 section into long ropes, about as thick as your pinky finger. Lightly spray with cooking spray to help prevent sticking.

6. Drop dumplings into boiling water and cook for 2-3 minutes. Toss with your sauce immediately, or rinse with cold water and store in a ziplock bag in the fridge for later.

Pictured is 3 points of cooked, store bought lasagna noodles, next to 3 points of cooked fresh pasta, made from a single 1/4 cup dough section. The fresh pasta sheet is approx. only 10 more calories, while being 3-4x the size.

This image shows the difference between 13 points of cooked of fresh linguini, next to 13 points of store bought spaghetti

- No Pasta Maker? No Problem:

Though it's ideal to try and make pasta with a pasta maker, you CAN make it without one. Sure, the finished pasta isn't uniform, but you'll definitely get your fit-points in while making it. Use a rolling pin to roll out the 1/4 cup sections of dough to be as wide/long/thin as you can. It won't be as great as with a machine, but it's doable. Dust your flat-ish dough with a little flour, using the wire strainer trick, then gently roll it into a long pinwheel. Use a sharp knife to cut thin slices into the rolled up dough. Once opened up, they will be long noodles.

- Minimize Points from Dusting:

When making your dough, try to not add too much liquid at once. Your goal is to have the dough just come together (for the regular pasta dough, not the gnocchi). Too wet, and you'll have to add more flour, which will up the points. As mentioned earlier, place 1-1/2 tsp of flour into a fine mesh wire strainer. If you HAVE to dust your dough, gently tap the strainer while holding it over your dough, so that it gets a very light dusting. That 1-1/2 tsp will last a long time this way. If the dough is a little too dry, spritz it with a light mist of olive oil cooking spray. Unlike water, it will add moisture while also helping it to avoid sticking.

- Freezing Dough:

I mention freezing extra 1 cup balls of dough. I'm usually asked how I freeze it and how long it lasts in the freezer. I wrap it in plastic wrap, then put that in a ziplock bag. I've thawed dough out 6 months later and used it. Haven't died yet. Wooot!

- 0 POINT PURPLE PLAN PASTA!

Use whole wheat, chickpea, or any type of NON-WHITE flour to make your fresh pasta, with this recipe, and it's 0 points under the purple plan.

Low Point Crust

Replacing Traditional Graham Cracker Crusts for Pies

One of the hardest things to manage while trying to eat healthier is desserts. Let's face it, it's the biggest hurdle for most of us, we love our sweets. Chief among those is pie, traditionally made with a ton of crushed graham crackers, sugar and butter. Regular Graham Cracker pie crust is a freaking Calorie Bomb, and as such is a ton of points. A typical graham cracker pie crust for a 9" pie will add around 55-70 points to your recipe, making it virtually impossible to have pies without blowing through all of your dailies. Well, you can still have pie crust, you just have to get creative and make some compromises.

As with all of this weird stuff I stumble upon, it's all born out of a desire to continue eating the foods I want, period. So, who would know how to knock the points from sugar and butter out of a dessert? Diabetics. I started searching through Diabetic cooking sites and forums and saw that they tended to use low sugar, high fiber cereals for their pie crusts instead of graham crackers. Turns out those are a lot less points than graham crackers too. After a few attempts, this is what I came up with.

Ingredients:

- 1-1/4 cups Kelloggs All Bran Cereal, All Bran Buds, Fiber One, or other low point High Fiber cereal
- 1/2 cup fat free plain Greek yogurt
- 3/4 tsp ground cinnamon
- 1-1/2 Tbsp sugar free maple syrup (pancake syrup)
- 4 second spray, butter flavored cooking spray (0 points worth, check your brand)
- 1/2 cup 0 point sweetener of choice (Monkfruit, Splenda, Stevia, etc)

Directions:

1. Put the cereal in a food processor, process on high until the cereal is ground into fine crumbs, resembling crushed graham crackers.
2. Add the remaining ingredients and process on high until well combined.
3. Spray a 9" pie pan or springform pan with cooking spray.
4. Press mixture down into pie pan and compress slightly. with your hands & fingers.
5. Cook the same as you would a regular graham cracker crust.

Points:		G	B	P
1 serving =		1	1	1
2 servings =		2	2	2
3 servings =		3	3	3

Servings:

- Makes enough crust for a 9 in. pie pan.
- 7 total points for the entire crust
- The above listed points, assume 8 servings.

COOKING TIPS:

- This crust is not as sweet as a regular graham cracker crusts. That's because regular graham crackers have enough sugar to make Paul Bunyan diabetic. After you prepare this mixture, taste it. Add more sweetener if you feel it needs to be sweeter.
- You can also consider adding some additional flavorings with baking extracts, such as vanilla, caramel, maple, or even pumpkin pie spice extract. They can be found in the spice aisle of your grocery store.
- Want it a little softer? Add some baking powder. Want it a little crisper? Add some baking soda and a splash of apple cider vinegar.

Dairy Free Pudding

Ever asked in Connect, a cooking forum, message board, facebook group, wherever... "Can you make pudding with Almond Milk?" and been met with an immediately dismissive "NO! It's impossible! Even Einstein couldn't figure it out!" Well, forget those Negative Nancys, they have no idea what they're talking about. You can make instant pudding with ANYTHING. Heck, in all of my pudding based frostings, I use cold water... so BOOM *mic drop*. It's suuuuuper easy and is extremely useful for cutting points when you're creating a recipe. It's also great for shaving a few extra calories off. Remember, a few calories here and there, add up over time. Summer's coming up and'ya want to look good in that leopard print speedo or tankini don't you?

Points:

The points are COMPLETELY dependent on what brand of pudding you buy (SCAN THE BOX), what dairy free liquid you use, as well as your application for the pudding. IE: Using it in a pie, eating it plain, parfait, etc. This page is just showing you how to make it.

Ingredients:

- Any brand of **INSTANT** pudding and pie filling
- Half as much fat free liquid as box-requested whole milk
  - Almond, Cashew, Soy Milk, etc.
  - Even COLD water works

Directions:

This is a truly simple food hack. All that is really required is the ability to pour liquid, use an electric hand mixer... and do 3rd grade math, unless you learned Common Core. Then, this simple math would require knowledge of Astro Physics. For this example, we're going to make instant butterscotch pudding, using cold water. Yes... water.

2. Mix, on high, for around 2 minutes, until the pudding gets thick and creamy. Store in the fridge, allowing more time to set. Done.

Notes:

- Using 1/2 as much fat free liquid, as the suggested milk, makes it a creamy pudding consistency. If you plan to use it for frosting, you'll need to make it thicker. Use less than 1/2. If the box calls for 2 cups of cold milk, use 3/4 cup of fat free liquid. If the box calls for 3 cups of milk, use 2-1/4 cups 0sp liquid.

1. In a mixing bowl or container, mix 1 packet of instant pudding and pie filling, with HALF AS MUCH water for the whole milk the instructions suggest. So for example, if the box says to use 3 cups of cold milk, use 1-1/2 cups of cold water or almond milk instead. Mix on high speed for 2-3 minutes.

Slow Cooker Roasted Garlic

Easy "Roasted" Garlic in your Slow Cooker

For those of you who are just starting out in the kitchen, or if you just simply haven't tried it before, I hope that I can convert you to the glories of Roasted Garlic. Where regular raw garlic has a sharp bite to it, Roasted Garlic is Raw Garlic's cool cousin that pulls up riding a Harley and blasting "Born In The USA". It has a deep flavor that is much smoother than regular garlic. It's "bite" is so mild that you can even eat it on its own, like macho candy, without flinching.

As a busy dad who has errands to run, roasting garlic in the oven isn't always practical, so doing it in the slow cooker is perfect. Throw a bunch of garlic in, come back 6 hours later, done.

Points: P
Total = 0 0 0

What You'll Need:

- Slow Cooker
- Whole Heads of Raw Garlic, as many as you want
- Aluminum Foil Wrap
- Olive Oil Cooking Spray
- Pinch of Salt
- Commercial-grade gas mask (optional)

Directions:

1. On a cutting board, use a knife to cut off the top 1/4 to 1/2 inch (depending on size of the garlic) from the top of each head. Remove some of the flaky papery skin from around the garlic.

2. Make an aluminum foil pouch that's at least 2 layers thick (a large piece of foil folded in half, to help avoid burning) and large enough to contain all of the cut heads of garlic.

3. Spray 5 times into the pouch with the olive oil cooking spray, coating all of the heads in a thick layer, then close the foil pouch. Leave a small slit or two.

4. Place a small cup or dish on the bottom of your slow cooker, and then place your foil pouch on top of it to help reduce the chance of burning. Cover and cook on the LOW setting for 6 hours.

5. Remove Garlic from the slow cooker and allow it to cool on a cutting board until you can handle it with your bare fingers. Careful, it's hot. Squeeze the soft garlic out of the skins, and store in a plastic ziplock bag in the freezer. Break off a few cloves whenever you need some. They thaw very quickly once removed from the freezer.

Notes:

- Regular Roasted Garlic recipes call for a good amount of olive oil to be poured over the garlic. Using my way, you get fat free, 0sp deliciously mellow and nutty garlic, without guilt.

- I prefer to have my slow cooker make this in my back yard. If you cook this inside your house for 6 hours your house will smell like a pizza parlor for days.

- Studies have shown that roasting garlic in this manner helps to prevent Vampire nests from forming on/near your property.

- Eating lots of garlic has been shown to work as a repellent for unwanted harassment and physical advances.

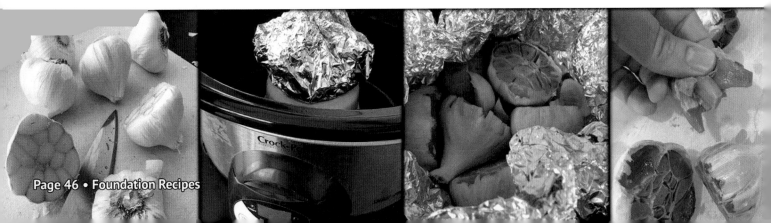

You So Spicy

Toasting & Blooming Spices, Seeds and ..... Stuff

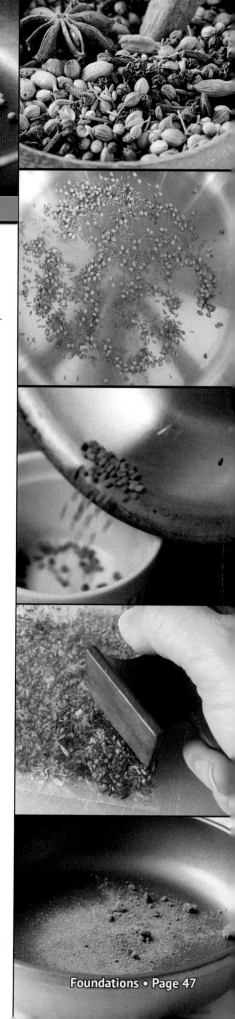

Though only 1 of the recipes in this cooking guide calls for toasting seeds or spices (Mexican Mole' sauce), this technique WILL be used in later cookbook volumes. Toasting spices and herbs enhances the flavors of some of my ground meat seasonings, as well as any of my sauces, dips and dressings that call for spices. You can toast whole spices, like fennel, caraway & coriander seeds. You can then use them whole, crush them, or you can buy an inexpensive spice grinder (I got mine for $8 on amazon) for fresh ground spices.

Aside from whole spices, you can "bloom" ground spices and even fresh herbs, like sprigs of rosemary and thyme. It's virtually the same process, but with ground spices and herbs. Other recipes, later on, will use toasted seeds, shredded coconut and more.

What You'll Need:

- A Pan
- Some Heat
- Seeds, Spices, Nuts, Herbs *(the legal kind, please)* and more
- A Fully Functioning Sniffer

Directions - Whole Spices:

1 Preheat a small pan over medium-low heat for around 30 seconds.
2 Add the amount of spices that you'll need into the pan. Shake it or stir the spices to prevent burning. Smaller spices and spices with thin skins need just a minute.
3 Once the spices become fragrant, remove them from the pan. If you plan to crush or grind your spices, allow them to cool first. Done.

Directions - Ground Spices (blooming):

1 Preheat a small pan over medium-low heat for around 30 seconds. For 0 point blooming, spray butter or olive oil cooking spray into the pan. Allow the spray to heat up a little bit, then add your ground spices to it and stir with a rubber spatula or wooden spoon, to form a paste. Lower the heat to low, ground spices can burn faster than whole.
2 Stir the spices to prevent burning. Once the paste become fragrant, add it to your dish.

Directions - Everything Else:

1 Pretty much the same as either of the above methods, just use common sense.
2 Use the "whole spice" method for toasting pine nuts, sesame seeds, peppercorns, wandering gnomes that you might find in your travels...

Note:

- You can add freshy sprigs of rosemary, thyme and other herbs to a hot pan to make them more fragrant, prior to adding them into a dish, though it does cause them to wilt slightly.
- Crush toasted seeds by placing them in a ziplock bag, then playing whack-a-mole with a kitchen malet, a small pot, or a CVS Pharmacy receipt.
- If you don't mind the extra points, you can use butter or oil to bloom your spices, but adjust your recipe's points accordingly.
- You can bloom your ground spices without any oil, spray, or liquids. Add the ground spices to the hot pan and stir as you would whole spices. It will take longer, but it works.

Yeast Slider Buns

Deliciously dense, yet fluffy and light, slider buns

This is my first TRUE success at perfectly sized and shaped yeast slider buns. Unlike 2 ingredient dough, which ends up always tasting like a biscuit, these buns have a great texture, similar to a dense (yet fluffy) loaf of bread. Real sugar is a necessity in this recipe, for the yeast to rise. The yeast won't do it's voodoo with artificial sweeteners, sorry... I tried. These are definitely worth the little bit of time it takes to make them and as an added bonus, you can use this recipe to make full sized burger patties, by using 1/4 or 1/3 cup sections of the dough, to make your buns, rather than 1/8 sections.

		G	B	P
Servings Info.:	**Points:**	1 serving =	2 2 2
Yield: 8 buns		2 servings =	4 4 4
Serving Size: 1 bun		3 servings =	6 6 6

Ingredients:

Egg Dough, Slider Buns
- 1 cup self rising flour
- 4 tsp sugar (1 tsp for yeast, 3 tsp in flour)
- 2 tsp active dry yeast (found in the baking/spice aisle)
- 1/4 cup very warm water (around 100 degrees)
- additional water, 3-4 Tbsp for mixing
- Cooking spray (i like butter flavored, but that's just me)
- 1 large egg + 1 tsp water for egg wash

Egg Wash (OPTIONAL)**
- 1 large egg + 1 tsp water for egg wash

Directions:

1. Scoop the active dry yeast, and 1 teaspoon of sugar, into a tall container or cup. Take 1/4 cup of aaaalmost hot water, around 100 degrees (right around where it feels too hot on your hand to fill a kid's bathtub with), then stir the 1/4 cup of semi hot water into the container and stir. Any hotter than 110 degrees and you'll kill the yeast. Stir the water gently to mix the ingredients, then allow to sit, untouched, for 10 minutes. It will foam up, a LOT.

 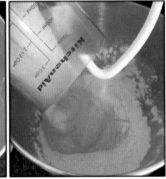

2. Place the flour and remaining 3 teaspoons of sugar into a large mixing bowl. After the yeast has "bloomed" for 10 minutes (pictured in step 1b), pour the yeast water into the flour.

3. Begin mixing the dry and wet ingredients. The mixture will be very dry and you'll need to add more warm water. It took me 3-4 additional Tablespoons of water for it all to JUST form a dough ball. You want the dough to require as little extra liquid as possible. Ideally, you want it to end up with the consistency of firm play dough. If it's a little tacky, lightly spray it all around with cooking spray, problem solved. Lightly spray a cutting board with cooking spray, then get to work.

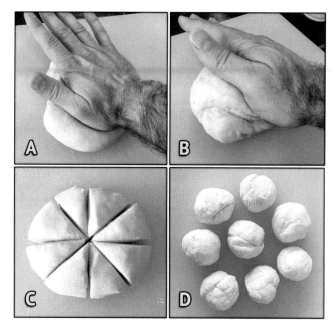

4. (A) Push down on the dough with your palm, then (B) fold the dough over and push down again. Repeat the folding process 20 times, then roll the dough back into a large ball. (C) Cut the ball into 8 equal sections, then (D) roll the cut sections into balls. Spray with cooking spray if the dough is tacky.

7. Use a kitchen brush (or paper towel) to lightly coat the risen dough, with egg wash. Bake at 350 for 12 minutes, then immediately turn up the heat to 450 and continue baking for an additional 3 minutes, or till just beginning to turn golden brown. Remove from oven to cool.

Notes:

- If you are allergic to gluten, you can make this recipe with gluten free flour. Bob's Red Mill has a really good Gluten Free All Purpose flour, that's available in many major supermarkets. Make sure to adjust your points, if necessary..
- These buns are the foundation of every single one of my slider recipes. Use these buns for every one, unless you choose to use the pretzel buns instead. Some of the slider recipes call for additional spices to be added to the the buns for that recipe.
- To make regular sized buns, cut the 1 cup dough balls into three 1/3 dough balls. Let them rise for 20 minutes, rather than 10. Then bake as directed.
- The egg wash is a completely optional step, just to give them a more golden appearance. I did NOT add the point for the egg wash into the Green plan's points, because it's optional. If you use it, adjust your points.

5. Line a sheet pan with parchment paper paper. Roll each 1/8 dough section into a smooth ball in your palm. Place each ball onto the pan and do NOT push down on them. Try your best to keep them in a rounded ball shape. If your dough is too wet, the buns will become flattened, rather than rounded, while baking. Spray the tops of the balls with cooking spray, then walk away and allow the dough to rise for 20 mins. Preheat your oven to 350.

6. In a small dish, whisk 1 large egg and 1 teaspoon of water together, to make an egg wash.

Pretzel Slider Buns

Moist, Soft, Fluffy, De-Freakin-Licious "Pretzel" Buns

This is a variation of my standard Yeast Bun recipe from the previous page. However, rather than baking these, we're first going to boil them first, then bake them. That quick boil makes a HUGE difference with the texture, once baked. They end up tasting like a soft, doughy, chewy pretzel. Errrr-Ma-Gaaaawd, they are good!

		G	B	P
Servings Info.:	**Points:** 1 serving =	2	2	2
Yield: 8 buns	2 servings =	4	4	4
Serving Size: 1 bun	3 servings =	6	6	6

Ingredients:

Egg Dough, Slider Buns
- 1 cup self rising flour
- 4 tsp sugar (1 tsp for yeast, 3 tsp in flour)
- 2 tsp active dry yeast (found in the baking/spice aisle)
- 1/4 cup very warm water (around 100 degrees)
- additional water, 3-4 Tbsp for mixing
- Cooking spray (i like butter flavored, but that's just me)
- 1 large egg + 1 tsp water for egg wash *(OPTIONAL)*

Water Bath
- big pot o' water
- 1/2 cup baking soda (for boiling water)

Directions:

1. Scoop the active dry yeast, and 1 teaspoon of sugar, into a tall container or cup. Take 1/4 cup of aaaalmost hot water, around 100 degrees (right around where it feels too hot on your hand to fill a kid's bathtub with), then stir the 1/4 cup of semi hot water into the container and stir. Any hotter than 110 degrees and you'll kill the yeast. Stir the water gently to mix the ingredients, then allow to sit, untouched, for 10 minutes. It will foam up, a LOT.

2. Place the flour and remaining 3 teaspoons of sugar into a large mixing bowl. After the yeast has "bloomed" for 10 minutes (pictured in step 1b), pour the yeast water into the flour.

3. Begin mixing the dry and wet ingredients. The mixture will be very dry and you'll need to add more warm water. It took me 3-4 additional Tablespoons of water for it all to JUST form a dough ball. You want the dough to require as little extra liquid as possible. Ideally, you want it to end up with the consistency of firm play dough. If it's a little tacky, lightly spray it all around with cooking spray, problem solved. Lightly spray a cutting board with cooking spray, then get to work.

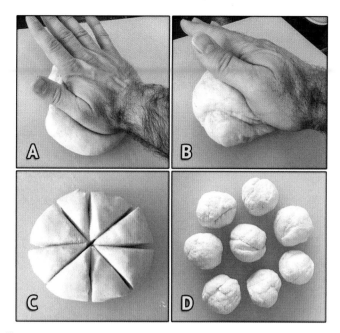

5. **(A)** Push down on the dough with your palm, then **(B)** fold the dough over and push down again. Repeat the folding process 20 times, then roll the dough back into a large ball. **(C)** Cut the ball into 8 equal sections, then **(D)** roll the cut sections into balls. Spray with cooking spray if the dough is tacky.

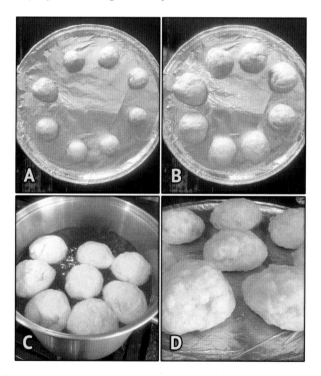

6. Preheat your oven to 450 degrees, for later.
   (A) Prep a baking pan with foil and cooking spray. Place the 8 dough balls onto the baking sheet, spaced apart, then gently press down on them, just a little bit, to flatten the tops slightly. Spray them with cooking spray. **(B)** Turn the heat back up on your pot of water, so it goes back up to a boil. Meanwhile, Let the dough balls rise for **ONLY** 10 minutes. **(C)** Carefully place all 8 dough balls into the boiling water. Boil for 30 seconds, then flip and boil for another 30 seconds. **(D)** Remove from the water, with a slotted spoon and return to your baking sheet.

7. Lightly spray the top of each bun with butter flavored cooking spray then bake at 450 degrees for 13-16 minutes, or until the buns are dark brown. all around. Done.

Notes:
- If you are allergic to gluten, you can make this recipe with gluten free flour. Bob's Red Mill has a wide range of Gluten Free flours, that are available in many major supermarkets.
- To make regular sized buns, cut the 1 cup dough balls into three 1/3 dough balls. Let them rise for 15 minutes, rather than 10. Then boil and bake as directed.
- If you want your pretzel buns to have salt on top, sprinkle the tops with coarse kosher salt before they go in the oven.

Yeast Pizza Dough

A Simple Airy & Crisp Yeast-Based Pizza Dough Recipe

A simple and basic Yeast-Based recipe that will let you make delicious thin or thick crust pizzas, calzones, baked bread bowls, bread sticks and much more. Making yeast dough sounds much more intimidating than it really is. It's great for when you will be home for a while and have some chores, or need to run errands away from the kitchen for an hour or two. It's great for a busy multi-tasking kinda day.

Points: G B P
Entire Crust = 14   14   14

Ingredients:

- 1 cup All Purpose Flour (or your flour of choice)
- 1/4 tsp Salt (optional if on low sodium diet)
- 1/4 tsp Baking Powder
- 1-1/2 tsp Active Dry Yeast
- 1 tsp Sugar
- 1/2 cup hot Water, between 100-110 degrees

Directions:

1. Combine the flour, salt and baking powder in a large mixing bowl. Set aside

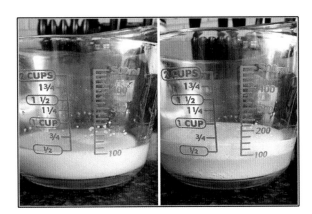

2. In another dish or cup, pour in the active dry yeast and sugar. Pour in the 1/2 cup of (not too hot) hot water then stir for a few seconds to mix. Allow the yeast water to sit untouched for 15 minutes. In that time the water will develop a frothy "head" to it.

3. After 15 minutes, pour the yeast mixture into the mixing bowl with the dry ingredients. Mix to combine until a dough ball is formed, adding a bit more water if the mix is still too dry. It's ok if it's a little sticky.

4. Lightly spray a bowl with cooking spray and put the dough ball in, then cover the bowl with plastic wrap. Walk away and allow the dough to rise for 30 minutes. By that time, it will have expanded and fluffed up a bit.

5. Remove the dough and place it onto the center of a pizza pan that has been lightly sprayed with cooking spray. Stretch out the dough to a large round shape, spray the top with cooking spray and allow it to rest for 1 hour uncovered.

6. After 1 hour the dough has risen a good deal, lightly spray the dough with olive oil cooking spray and gently stretch it more.

7. Put your sauce, cheese and toppings onto the pizza and allow it one final rest for 30 minutes. Turn on your oven to 400.

8. After your pizza has had the additional 30 minutes to rise and has been topped, get ready to put it into your preheated oven.

9. Lightly spray the visible crust with cooking spray, then put your pizza in the oven and bake at 400 degrees for 16-20 minutes. Ovens vary, so yours may take a longer.

10. Bask in the glory of real pizza dough.

COOKING IDEAS:

- If you make a double batch of this dough you can make an AWESOME deep dish pizza in a 13"x9" casserole pan, using the exact same method listed to make this dough, just with the doubled ingredients.

- If you make a double batch you can also put your dough onto a large baking sheet pan rather than a round pizza pan, roll the dough into a long rectangular shape, then allow it to rise, stretch it more, rise, top it, bake it and you can get up to 18 good sized square slices out of it.

- You can use instant yeast instead of dry active yeast. Rather than adding the active dry yeast to water and waiting 10 minutes as stated in these directions, you can simply add 2-1/2 tsp of instant yeast directly into the flour with the warm water and mix the dough. It will rise when you let the dough ball rest. It saves a little time.

- You can use this to make Calzones, Strombolis, life sized edible statues of your pets... get creative.

- I personally like to add 1/2 tsp of garlic powder, 1/2 tsp of onion powder, 1 tsp of dried thyme and some cracked black pepper into the flour. The finished bread can be used as breadsticks or for paninis.

Black Peppercorn - pg 62

Asian Glaze - pg. 56
mixed with BBQ Sauce - pg. 58

Pesto - pg. 75

Bearnaise - pg. 59

Section Recipes

Low Point, Calorie & Fat, Sauce Recipes

SAUCES

(yeah, it's not a sauce, but you deserve Hummus)

Asian Glaze & Dipping Sauce

A thick and sticky dipping sauce that's easily customizable

This is a very simple Asian inspired sauce that can easily be docked up with additional spices and flavorings for your own preferences. This sauce is yummie as listed, but can be kicked up a few notches by adding lemongrass, some lime juice, honey, sugar free bbq sauce, or any number of additional flavors.

Ingredients:

- 4 Tbsp less sodium soy sauce
- 2 Tbsp 0 point sweetener of choice (monkfruit, stevia, etc)
- 1/4 tsp molasses**
- 1 medium garlic clove, minced (1tsp)
- 1/4 tsp ground ginger
- 2 Tbsp tomato sauce
- 2 Tbsp sugar free pancake syrup**
- 2 Tbsp rice wine vinegar
- 1-1/4 cups Water
- 4-1/2 tsp cornstarch (dissolved into the water)
- 1/2 tsp asian chili sauce, or more, to taste

Serving Info.:

Yields: 2 cups
Servings: 8
Serving Size: 1/4 cup

Points:

	G	B	P
1 serving =	0	0	0
2 servings =	1	1	1
3 servings =	1	1	1
4 servings =	1	1	1

Directions:

1. Dissolve the cornstarch with the water, then heat ALL of the ingredients in a small pot, over medium-high heat, till boiling.
2. Reduce heat, continue cooking at a boil low boil for 3-4 minutes, till it begins to coat the back of a spoon.
3. Remove sauce from heat, pour into a bowl and set aside. It will thicken as it cools.
4. Stir sauce again after 5 minutes off of heat, serve warm or cold.

Notes:

- If you have access to 0 point brown sugar substitute, swap the 2 Tbsp of sweetener and 1/4 tsp of molasses, with 2 Tbsp of 0 point brown sugar substitute.
- You can use regular pancake syrup if you want, but adjust your points
- If you don't want to buy rice wine vinegar, use regular distilled white vinegar, it'll work just fine.
- Adding 1/4 tsp of sesame oil REALLY kicks the sauce up, without adding any points.
- You can also use my hack for DIY 0 point "Honey", from the ingredient swap section, in place of the sugar free syrup, for a more authentic asian flavor. Boil 1/2 cup of water with some sweetener, 1-1/2 tsp dissolved cornstarch, and some honey extract, or even simply add honey extract to the sugar free syrup.

Avocado Cilantro Sauce

A deliciously creamy sauce perfect for meats, veggies and even salads

This velvety smooth avocado dressing is a tasty mix of herbs, creaminess, citrus and savoriness. It is just at home on tacos and fish as it is being used for a salad dressing. This is an extremely simple sauce because all that is required is a food processor or a large blender to puree the mixture. The reason we're able to get an entire 1/4 cup serving of this Avocado sauce for 1 point is that we are being smart with our ingredients. We're stretching out the Avocado with water, broth and greek yogurt to get a lot more servings out of it which decreases the points per serving.

The end result is a sauce that is creamy and smooth with a subtle lime flavor, a healthy dose of cilantro and a delicious richness from the Avocado.

Serving Info.:
YIELDS: 2-1/2 cups
Servings: 10
Serving Size: 1/4 cup

Points:

	G	B	P
1 serving =	1	1	1
2 servings =	3	2	2
3 servings =	4	3	3
4 servings =	6	4	4

Ingredients:

- 1 medium Avocado
- 2 medium garlic cloves
- 1 cup fresh cilantro
- 3 Tbsp lime juice
- 1/2 cup water
- 1/2 cup chicken broth
- 1 cup plain fat free greek yogurt
- 1/2 tsp salt
- 1/4 tsp pepper
- Olive oil spray, 5 second spray

Directions:

1. Carefully slice the avocado in half, remove the pit and skin, then place the avocado into the food processor.
2. Add all of the remaining ingredients to the food processor and then puree on high speed for around 1 minute, or until all of the ingredients are broken down and smooth.
3. Season with additional salt and pepper, if necessary.
4. Serve immediately or chill in the refrigerator.

Notes:

- This is more of a savory sauce than a bright citrus one. If you would prefer it to have a less savory taste, then replace the chicken broth with additional water. Do not add any pepper, and only season with a minimal amount of salt, to taste, after the rest of the ingredients are finished being pureed.
- Add more water to thin the mixture, if you want a thinner sauce/dressing
- Go ahead and use 1 tsp of regular olive oil instead of the cooking spray, if you wish. Make sure to adjust your points though.

Barbecue Sauce

A simple sauce that you can easily modify and build off of

Brush this simple sugar free barbecue sauce on chops, kebabs or chicken drumsticks before cooking, or use as a glaze during grilling. Serve it as either a hot or cold sauce to go with any of your favorite dishes. It's a perfect base to dock up yourself for a low point bbq style sauce. It's so low in points that you have a lot of room to play around with adding ingredients to make it your own.

Ingredients:

- 1/4 cup water
- 2 large onions, chopped
- 4 garlic cloves, medium, chopped
- 1 (29oz) can of tomato sauce (the 0 point kind)
- 1/4 cup worcestershire sauce
- 2 Tbsp apple cider vinegar
- 1/4 cup sugar free maple syrup
- 2 Tbsp 0 point sweetener o' choice
  (*Monkfruit, Stevia, Swerve, Splenda, etc*)
- 2 tsp ground mustard
- 1/2 tsp onion powder
- 1 tsp chili powder
- 3/4 tsp smoked paprika
- 1 tsp paprika
- 1 tsp molasses (OPTIONAL, but recommended)
- 1/2 tsp liquid smoke, hickory or mesquite (OPTIONAL)
- 1-2 canned chipotle peppers in adobo sauce (OPTIONAL)
- salt and pepper to taste

Serving Info.:

Yields: 5 cups
Servings: 20
Serving Size: 1/4 cup

Points: G B P

	G	B	P
1 serving =	0	0	0
2 servings =	0	0	0
3 servings =	1	1	1
4 servings =	1	1	1
5 servings =	1	1	1

Directions:

1 In a medium saucepan, saute the onions and garlic with cooking spray, until softened.
2 Stir in all of the remaining ingredients and heat to a low simmer.
3 Cover and simmer for 15 minutes.
4 Pour the mixture into a blender or food processor and process on high until smooth.
5 Return the sauce to the pan and season with additional salt and pepper, if desired.

Variations:
- *This recipe is so low in points that it leaves you a lot of room to customize it, while staying low point.*
- *Want a southwest kick? Add the optional canned chipotle pepper in adobo sauce prior to pureeing.*
- *The molasses is optional, but it does add a little depth. If you don't mind the 2nd serving going up to 1 point, add some more. Remember, use this as a base to customize your own bbq sauce from.*
- *MAKE SURE YOU SCAN YOUR TOMATO SAUCE. It's probably a glitch, but I've had some canned tomato sauce (walmart brand, recently) scan as 0 points, but then SAVE in my recipe as up to 11 points. Crazy.*

Bearnaise Sauce

A Classic French Herbed Wine Sauce For Meat Eaters

A classic French sauce gets a low point makeover in this lightened version of one of the most classic French "mother" sauces. Typically, it is made with an emulsion of egg yolk, white wine, vinegar, herbs and loooots of butter. This sauce is Hollandaise's sophisticated wine drinking older brother.

Ingredients:

- 5 Tbsp white wine vinegar
- 1 Tbsp white wine, chardonnay
- 1 cup water
- 1 small onion, chopped
- 4 second spray, butter flavored cooking spray (0 points)
- 1 bay leaf
- a few sprigs each of fresh parsley and tarragon
- 1/4 tsp cracked black pepper
- 1-1/2 Tbsp I Can't Believe It's Not Butter Light
- 1 tsp cornstarch, dissolved in a little bit of water, set aside
- 3 large egg yolks
- 1 Tbsp finely chopped fresh parsley
- 1 Tbsp finely chopped fresh tarragon

Serving Info.:

Yields: 2 cups
Servings: 8
Serving Size: 1/4 cups

Points:

	G	B	P
1 serving =	1	0	0
2 servings =	2	1	1
3 servings =	3	1	1
4 servings =	4	2	2

Directions:

1. Combine the white wine, vinegar, water, chopped onion, bay leaf, pepper, butter spray, butter spread and the sprigs of fresh herbs in a small stock pot and heat until boiling. Lower the heat to medium/low and keep at a low simmer for 5 minutes.

2. Pour the mixture through a wire strainer and into a bowl, to remove all of the vegetables and herbs. Set the bowl of strained liquid aside and allow to cool for 30 minutes.

3. After cooling for 30 minutes, return the mixture to your sauce pot and whisk in the egg yolks and dissolved cornstarch. Turn on the stove to medium and heat until the sauce begins to warm and thicken, about 5 minutes, stirring with a rubber spatula.

4. Once the sauce comes to a low simmer, reduce the heat to barely simmering and allow to continue cooking for 3 minutes, continue stirring.

5. Pour the thickened sauce into a bowl and stir in the chopped fresh parsley and tarragon. Can be served as a hot or cold sauce.

Bechamel Sauce

A deliciously light and versatile take on a classic French sauce

Bechamel is a creamy base sauce, typically loaded with heavy cream and butter. We are using unsweetened almond milk and I can't believe it's not butter Light, cooked with vegetables and herbs to create a simple sauce with a subtle depth of flavor. It has an excellent mellow base, which makes it ideal for lasagnas, as well as an accompaniment for many fish, egg, and vegetable dishes. It can also be used as a base in a wide range of sauces and dishes. Add some garlic and you have a creamy garlic sauce, add lemon and herbs and you have a creamy lemon and herb sauce, the possibilities are endless. I personally like to use it for the white sauce in my low point chicken and vegetable lasagna pictured to the left. It is a much healthier WW-ified take on a major brand's frozen vegetable lasagna that we all know and love.

Ingredients:

- 1/2 cup unsweetened almond milk
- 3 cups water
- 1 Tbsp I can't believe it's not butter Light
- butter flavored cooking spray, 5-6 seconds spray (0 points)
- 1 tsp chicken flavored bouillon (granules)
- 1 pinch of nutmeg
- 2-3 sprigs of fresh parsley
- 2-3 sprigs of fresh rosemary or thyme
- 1 small onion, chopped
- 1 medium carrot, peeled and chopped
- 1 celery stalk, chopped
- 1 bay leaf
- 1/4 cup plain fat free Greek yogurt
- 4 Tbsp cornstarch, mixed into the Greek yogurt
- 1/2 tsp salt
- black or white pepper, to taste

Servings:

Makes: 3 cups
Servings: 6
Serving Size: 1/2 cup

Points: Ⓖ Ⓑ Ⓟ

	G	B	P
1 serving =	1	1	1
2 servings =	1	1	1
3 servings =	2	1	1
4 servings =	2	2	2

Notes:

- Use any type of butter you want, but adjust points accordingly. I am using 1 point of I can't believe it's not butter Light, in this recipe.
- If you would prefer to use actual broth instead of the chicken flavored granules, leave out the granules/bouillon and replace 1 cup of the water with 1 cup of vegetable stock. Adjust points the points if necessary.

Directions:

1. Dice the onion, carrot and celery. Spray a medium stock pot with the butter flavored cooking spray and cook the veggies on medium heat for 3-4 minutes, until they begin to sweat.
2. Pour in the water, milk, butter spread, bouillon, nutmeg, along with the fresh herbs and bay leaf. Bring to a boil, over medium heat, then remove the pot from the heat and allow the mixture to steep for 30 minutes.
3. Pour the cooled mixture through a strainer, into a bowl, to remove the vegetables.
4. In a separate bowl, combine the cornstarch and yogurt until smooth, adding a little bit of the sauce to warm up the Greek.
5. Pour the strained liquid back into the pot and stir in the yogurt/cornstarch mixture, until smooth.
6. Heat the mixture over medium heat, stirring frequently, until it reaches a low boil. Reduce the heat and allow to barely simmer for 3-4 minutes for the sauce to thicken up a bit.
7. Remove the pan from the heat and season to taste with pepper.
8. The sauce can be served immediately, or it can be allowed to cool for a few minutes. It thickens more as it cools.

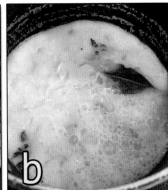

Bechamel Variations

NOTE: All Bechamel variation recipes have the same 1/4 cup serving size as the original bechamel sauce.

Bechamel is a perfect base for a number of creamy, savory sauces. You can make 1 batch of Bechamel and easily modify it for your own tastes with just a few minor tweaks. For all of these sauces, make a regular batch of Bechamel sauce with the listed changes and additions. This'll show you how easy it is to make your own creations.

Alfredo Sauce:

Prepared by: @ leesha_jay

Recipe Changes:

- Add 3 chopped cloves of garlic to the vegetables in the first step of the Bechamel sauce.
- Stir in 1/4 cup of reduced fat Parmesan grated topping. (such as Kraft reduced fat Parmesan)

Points:

	G	B	P
1 serving =	1	1	1
2 servings =	2	2	2
3 servings =	3	2	2

Lemon & Chive Cream Sauce:

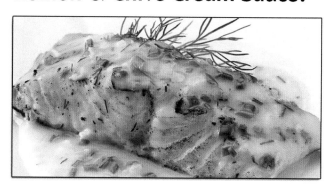

Recipe Changes:

- Use a small bunch of chopped fresh chives in place of the Rosemary or Thyme during the first steps of making your Bechamel sauce. Strain as normal.
- Add 2 Tbsp of lemon juice and 3 Tbsp of fresh chopped chives to the finished sauce

Points:

	G	B	P
1 serving =	1	1	1
2 servings =	1	1	1
3 servings =	2	1	1

Creamy Herb Sauce:

Prepared by: @ mugglemama2017

Tarragon Sage Chicken with Butternut Squash Soup and Tarragon Sage Cream

Recipe Changes:

- Replace the rosemary or thyme in the Bechamel sauce with any other herb, such as dill, tarragon, sage, basil, cilantro, etc. and remove during straining.
- Stir in more finely chopped fresh herbs to the sauce at step 7, when it is completely finished cooking and removed from heat.

Points:

	G	B	P
1 serving =	1	1	1
2 servings =	1	1	1
3 servings =	2	1	1

Roasted Garlic Cream Sauce:

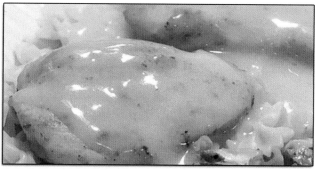

Recipe Changes:

- Add 5-6 medium sized cloves of roasted garlic (pg 33) to all of the vegetables when making the Bechamel. Also, add 1-1/2 tsp garlic powder and 1-1/2 Tbsp reduced fat grated parmesan topping (like Kraft parmesan topping). Strain out the garlic cloves along with the other vegetables.

Points:

	G	B	P
1 serving =	1	1	1
2 servings =	1	1	1
3 servings =	3	2	2

Black Peppercorn Sauce

A smoky black pepper cream sauce with delicious depth

This sauce tastes so good! It has a savory herbed butter flavor with a smoky pepperiness that sneaks up and karate chops the back of your tongue like an angry creamy ninja. This would be absolutely awesome on beef and pork. Heck, it'd be good as lip balm for goodness sake.

Ingredients:

- 1 Tbsp I Can't Believe It's Not Butter Light
- 1 small onion, finely diced
- 2 medium cloves garlic, crushed and finely chopped
- 1/2 tsp salt
- 5 sprays, butter flavored cooking spray
- 1 bay leaf
- 3-4 sprigs fresh thyme
- 2-1/2 tsp black pepper (coarse if able)
- 2-1/2 tsp whole black peppercorns
- 1/2 cup unsweetened plain almond milk
- 4-1/2 tsp cornstarch (mixed into the almond milk)
- 1/2 cup chicken broth
- 3/4 cup water
- 2 tsp lemon juice

Serving Info.:

Yields: 2 cups
Servings: 8
Serving Size: 1/4 cups

Points:

	G	B	P
1 serving =	1	1	1
2 servings =	1	1	1
3 servings =	1	1	1
4 servings =	1	1	1

Directions:

1. Melt the butter spread in a pan and cook onions for 3-4 minutes, until sweating. Add the garlic and cook for 1-2 minutes, until it becomes fragrant.
2. Spray the onions and garlic for 5 seconds with butter flavored cooking spray, add the herbs, black pepper and peppercorns to the pan and cook on medium-low heat for 3-4 minutes.
3. In a separate bowl, whisk together the almond milk and cornstarch, then add the chicken broth, water and lemon juice.
4. Pour the liquid mixture into the pan with the onions and pepper, stir constantly with a whisk. Bring the sauce up to a low boil and continue stirring for 3-4 minutes, until it thickens to your desired consistency. Use a fork to remove and discard the thyme leaves and bay leaf.
5. Turn off the heat and serve immediately, or allow to cool for a few minutes. The sauce thickens more as it cools.

Notes:

- You can replace the almond milk with any type of milk you want, but adjust points accordingly.
- This would be great with sauteed mushrooms added into it, which would have the added benefit of "bulking up" the sauce. Doing so would not just taste great, but it would both increase the servings and possibly lower the points for the first serving.
- If you'd like to add a little bit more savory depth of flavor to the sauce, you can stir in up to 1-1/2 teaspoons of reduced fat parmesan topping (like Kraft) into the sauce, for 0 points. Then you can sound super snazzy, telling people you made a Parmesan Black Peppercorn Cream Sauce. Heck, this thing's so low in points, you can add more, just adjust the points.

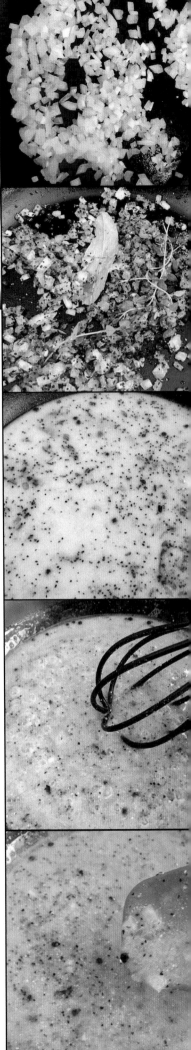

Bolognese & Ragu Sauces

An extremely hearty meat sauce originating from Bologna Italy

A traditional Bolognese sauce is a thing of beauty. Where a Marinara sauce is what you would typically think of when you picture a plate of spaghetti or on a pizza, a Bolognese sauce is much more hearty. The sauce is usually packed with ground beef or pork sausage, but we are going for a low fat, low calorie, low point sauce, so we are using my ultra low point, ultra flavorful 0 point italian sausage recipe from page 28. You can easily transform this into an equally delicious chunky ragu sauce, by tweaking the spices and not pureeing the vegetables. Want to make this even more filling? Add some mushrooms to get even more servings out of it.

Serving Info.:
Yields: 6 cups
Servings: 9
Serving Size: 2/3 cup

Points:

	G	B	P
1 serving =	1	0	0
2 servings =	2	1	1
3 servings =	4	1	1
4 servings =	5	1	1

Ingredients:

- 1 pound uncooked "0 point" Italian Sausage (page 28)
- 1 medium onion, diced (around 1-1/2 cups)
- 1/2 cup carrot, finely chopped***
- 1/2 cup celery, finely chopped***
- 4-5 medium garlic cloves, minced
- 2/3 cup low fat beef or chicken broth
- 1 Tbsp red wine vinegar
- 1/4 cup red wine
- 2 Tbsp tomato paste, no salt added
- 29 oz. canned tomato sauce (scan to ensure 0 points)
- 1/2 cup unsweetened plain almond milk **
- 1 tsp italian seasoning
- 1/2 tsp rosemary, minced
- 1/2 tsp ground allspice**
- 1/2 tsp ground nutmeg**
- salt and pepper to taste

NOTES:
- For a regular ragu sauce, DON'T puree the vegetables, leave the sauce chunky. Also, remove the almond milk, allspice and nutmeg.
- If you're allergic to almond milk, use ANYTHING YOU WANT... seriously, this recipe has less points than a Lakers game.

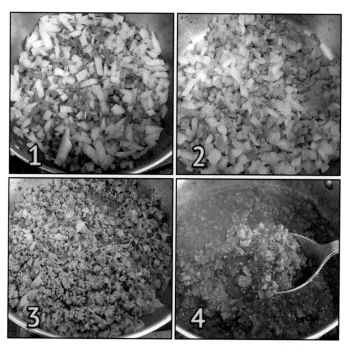

Directions: *(for Bolognese)*

1. Cook the onions, celery, carrots and garlic in a pot with olive oil cooking spray (a 0 point amount) for 5-6 minutes, until they begin to sweat.
2. Add the broth. Cook for 5-10 minutes, or until almost all of the liquid has reduced.
3. Add the raw "italian sausage" and cook till browned, breaking up the meat into small pieces, with a spoon.
4. Add the vinegar, wine, tomato paste, tomato sauce, almond milk, italian seasoning, rosemary allspice and nutmeg. Bring to a boil.
5. Reduce to low heat, then cover with a lid and cook at a low simmer, **COVERED**, for 30 minutes. Season to taste.

Serving Info.:

Yields: 1-3/4 cups
Servings: 7
Serving Size: 1/4 cup

Points:

	G	B	P
1 serving =	1	0	0
2 servings =	1	1	1
3 servings =	1	1	1
4 servings =	1	1	1

Buffalo Sauce

An addictively spicy hot sauce that holds the universe together

Good old Buffalo sauce, a Holy Union between cayenne pepper-based hot sauce, vinegar and lots and lots and lots of butter. It's one of those things that everyone enjoys, but that most people trying to cut calories have to avoid because of the fat content. Well, that was true until the heavens opened, the clouds parted, choirs of angels started singing and I bestowed this virtually fat free gift upon you all. Pretty much every single "skinny" food blogger does the same exact carbon copy recipe of, "Mix hot sauce with a bucket of Greek yogurt to make Buffalo sauce, Yippie!" Sorry, Susie... Homey don't play that way. I modify real recipes. Greek yogurt shouldn't be used as a crutch. Instead of using a bunch of butter, we're using a combination of butter flavored cooking spray, butter spread and a cup of water that's been thickened with cornstarch. Then, we pack in depth of flavor with vinegar, worcestershire, chicken granules and garlic powder.

Ingredients:

- 4 second spray, butter flavored cooking spray (only use 0 points, scan your can)
- 1 cup water
- 1 Tbsp cornstarch
- 3/4 cup Franks Red Hot Cayenne Pepper Sauce, Original
- 2 tsp worcestershire sauce
- 2 Tbsp white vinegar
- 1 Tbsp I can't believe it's not butter Light
- 1/8 tsp granulated garlic powder
- 1/4 tsp chicken flavored granules (trust me, just roll with it)
- 2 Tbsp plain fat free Greek yogurt

Directions:

1 Spray the butter flavored cooking spray into a small sauce pot, then add the water and cornstarch. Mix till the cornstarch is dissolved.
2 Add the hot sauce, worcestershire, vinegar, butter spread, garlic powder and the chicken flavored bouillon/granules. Cook over high heat until the sauce comes to a rolling boil, then lower the heat to medium. Cook at a low boil for 3 minutes.
3 Pour the sauce into a mixing bowl and allow to cool for 10 minutes.
4 Add the Greek yogurt, stir or whisk until the Greek yogurt has been completely incorporated into the sauce, without lumps. Done.

Note:

- This is a not a dip, this is a sauce, like you would toss wings in. If you want it to be as thick as a dip, add some more Greek yogurt to thicken and stretch it to more servings.
- If you DON'T want to dillute it with more Greek to become a dip, but DO want it thicker, add another 1-1/2 tsp of cornstarch. The first serving will go up 1 point.
- Allergic to dairy? Swap out the Greek for Tofu (*gasp* Ingredient swaps!!)
- On the **GREEN** plan? Remove 1 Tbsp of the Greek yogurt and the first serving will drop to 0 points, just like **BLUE** and **PURPLE**. Crazy.

Butter Sauce Base

If there is one thing that you'd NEVER think you'd be having on Weight Watchers, chances are it's a low point butter sauce. C'mon, we're talking about using beautiful, golden, liquid fat, for goodness sake. However, as with most recipes in this guide/book, a little bit of messing with ingredient swaps, and a little trial and error, will work wonders for your cooking, as well as your waist line.

This butter sauce is a faaaaaantastic base for you to use as the foundation for a lot of sauces of your own making. You can add some herbs, wine, capers, a little reduced fat Parmesan, whatever you'd like. As it's written below, this sauce is very tasty, but it is tailor made for you to customize. Plug the recipe into your recipe builder and begin adding some fresh herbs (tip: some herbs cost a point after a certain amount), spices, and other seasonings. This sauce base is a game changer for trying to make a TON of low point traditional sauces.

Ingredients:

- 4-5 seconds spray, butter flavored cooking spray
  (use a 0 point amount, scan your can/brand)
- 5 Tbsp I can't believe it's not butter Light
- 1-3/4 cup water
- 4 tsp cornstarch, dissolved into water
- 1/8 tsp turmeric (optional, for deeper color)
- 1/2 tsp chicken flavored granules/bouillon
- 1/8 tsp salt, or more to taste.

Directions:

1 Spray the cooking spray into a small stock pot, then melt the butter spread over medium heat.
2 Add the water/cornstarch, turmeric (if using) chicken bouillon and salt into the pot and stir to combine. Turn up the heat and bring to a boil.
3 Cook at a rolling boil for 4 minutes, remove from heat. Done.

Serving Info.:

Yields: 2 cups
Servings: 8
Serving Size: 1/4 cup

Points:

	G	B	P
1 serving =	1	1	1
2 servings =	2	2	2
3 servings =	3	3	3
4 servings =	4	4	4

Note:

- Though optional, the Turmeric gives a deep golden color to the butter sauce. If you would like your sauce to be a lighter yellow, don't add it.
- Different brands of butter flavored cooking spray are different points. If you use the generic database entry, in the app, it gains a point after 2-3 seconds. However, scan your can. Some brands let you go up to 8 or more seconds for 0 points. The brand that I used "albertson's signature" let's you coat a '57 Buick for a few points.
- The sauce will continue to thicken as it cools.
- If you want to add even more of a butter punch, you can add butter flavored popcorn sprinkles or butter extract, from the baking/spice aisle, next to the vanilla extract.
- This sauce would go great as a butter base for other sauces, or for a dipping sauce for lobster, crab, etc.

Cheese Sauce

A deliciously low point cheddar cheese base sauce

This page is devoted to all of you cheese heads out there. This is a very easy to make cheese sauce that is awesome on pretty much anything. It can be poured over a baked potato, tossed with pasta to make low point mac n cheese, the possibilities are pretty much endless. It's also extremely customizable and easy to dock up. This isn't as thick and goopy as the canned nacho cheese goop. If you want super thick, make the cheese dip from my cookbook. This is slightly thinner, with the viscosity of hot nacho cheese.

Servings Info.:
Yields: 3-1/4 cups
Servings: 13
Serving Size: 1/4 cup

Points:

	G	B	P
1 serving =	1	1	1
2 servings =	1	1	1
3 servings =	2	2	2
4 servings =	3	3	3

Ingredients:

- 2-1/4 cups water
- (1) 10-3/4oz can Campbell's "Healthy Request" Condensed Cheddar Cheese Soup.
- 1/2 tsp salt
- 1/2 tsp chicken flavored bouillon granules
- 1/8 tsp ground turmeric
- 2 slices velveeta original cheese slices, *(3 points worth)*
- 4-1/2 Tbsp cornstarch,

For Nacho Cheese Sauce add:
- 4oz can diced green chilis (mild, med., or hot), drained
- cayenne or chipotle chili powder, to taste

Directions:

1. In a medium sauce pot, stir together the water, soup, salt, chicken granules, turmeric, cheese slices and cornstarch. Turn on the heat and bring to a rolling boil. Lower the heat to keep the mixture at a rolling boil, without letting the sauce bubble over. Allow to cook at low boil for 5-6 minutes.
2. After 5-6 minutes, remove pot from heat and allow to cool for 10 minutes. The sauce will thicken slightly while it cools. Done

Notes:

- If you cannot find Molly McButter Fat Free CHEESE sprinkles, most major grocery stores stock flavored seasoning powders near their popcorn in the snack aisle. *Kernel Season's* popcorn seasoning mixes sells a Nacho Cheddar powder. It is salty, so leave out the salt from the regular recipe. Enter it into the recipe builder to adjust points if you are using that powder.
- For Nacho Cheese sauce, use cayenne pepper for plain ol' heat. Adding chipotle chili powder (McCormick's) adds a little smokiness as well as heat.
- 1 can of the condensed soup shows as more points in the recipe builder. However, if you remove the soup from the can and do the points according to the weight of the ACTUAL contents of the can, it is lower in points, and how we get it to 1 point, from doing the points by weight.
- For an even thicker, really goopy Nacho Cheese sauce, you can add up to 1 additional tablespoon of cornstarch and still keep the first serving at 1 point.

Cilantro Lime Sauce

A simple and zesty sauce that packs some Latin attitude

This sauce is so simple and comes together so quickly that it'll come as a total surprise the first time that you make it. The flavorful mix of chicken broth, lime juice, garlic, and a bunch of fresh cilantro makes this an incredibly savory sauce. It punches you in the face with a nice bit of lime, followed by a strong flavor of cilantro. It pairs very well with Latin themed dishes, served over fish, chicken, beef and heck, even cardboard would taste great slathered in this stuff.

Though I'm using I Can't Believe It's Not Butter Light in this recipe, I give directions in the notes at the bottom of the page for how to make it a 0 point sauce with 1 simple ingredient substitution.

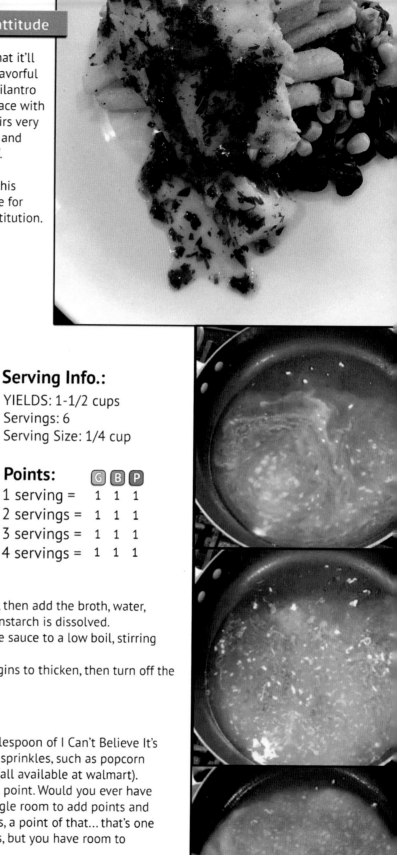

Ingredients:

- 5 second spray, Olive Oil cooking spray
- 1 cup chicken broth
- 1/4 cup water
- 2-1/2 tsp cornstarch, dissolved with a little water
- 1/4 tsp olive oil
- 3 Tbsp lime juice
- 2-3 medium cloves garlic, chopped
- 1 Tbsp I can't believe it's not butter Light
- 1 bunch fresh cilantro, finely chopped
- salt and pepper to taste

Serving Info.:

YIELDS: 1-1/2 cups
Servings: 6
Serving Size: 1/4 cup

Points: G B P

	G	B	P
1 serving =	1	1	1
2 servings =	1	1	1
3 servings =	1	1	1
4 servings =	1	1	1

Directions:

1 Spray the bottom of a medium pan with the cooking spray, then add the broth, water, cornstarch, olive oil, lime juice and garlic. Stir until the cornstarch is dissolved.
2 Add the butter spread, then turn on the stove and bring the sauce to a low boil, stirring to melt the butter spread.
3 Cook the sauce for 3-4 minutes at a rolling boil, until it begins to thicken, then turn off the heat and stir in the fresh chopped cilantro. Done.

Notes:

- For a 0 point version of this sauce simply replace the 1 Tablespoon of I Can't Believe It's Not Butter Light with a 0 point amount of "butter" flavored sprinkles, such as popcorn seasoning, Molly Mcbutter butter sprinkles, or Butter Buds (all available at walmart).
- Yes... you can seriously use an entire cup of this sauce for 1 point. Would you ever have an entire cup of sauce? No. But, that gives you a LOT of wiggle room to add points and customize this sauce for your own tastes. Add a point of this, a point of that... that's one of the reasons I make everything so low. It tastes good as-is, but you have room to modify my sauces.

Clam Sauce

A classic seafood sauce that's usually drenched in points

Servings:
- Yield: 4 cups
- Servings: 8
- Serving Size: 1/2 cup

Points:

	G	B	P
1 serving =	1	1	1
2 servings =	3	1	1
3 servings =	4	2	2
4 servings =	6	2	2

Linguini with White Clam Sauce is one of those staples of traditional southern italian cooking. It's one of those dishes that we all love or have wanted to try, but we shy away from it because of how much wine and butter are typically in it. After a member on Connect requested that I take a look at WW-ifying it, I was able to come up with an ultra low point, low calorie, virtually fat free version that is light, delicious and extremely flavorful. Not to mention that it's 1 point for a REALISTIC portion size, not 2 points for 2 measly little Tablespoons of sauce like you'll find elsewhere.

Ingredients:
- 4 sprays, butter flavored cooking spray
- 1 Tbsp I can't believe it's not butter Light
- 1/4 cup white wine, chardonnay
- 2 cups water
- 1/4 cup unsweetened almond milk
- 1/4 cup bottled clam juice
- 1 pinch red pepper flakes
- 5 garlic cloves, chopped (raw or roasted)
- 1 tsp chicken flavored bouillon granules
- 1 small onion, diced
- 2 (6oz) cans clams, chopped
- 2 Tbsp oregano, finely chopped
- 2 Tbsp parsley, finely chopped
- 2 Tbsp + 1 tsp cornstarch
- 1/4 tsp olive oil

Directions:
1 Spray the cooking spray into a medium pot, then add the butter spread, wine, water, almond milk, clam juice, pepper flakes, garlic, chicken granules diced onion and cornstarch. Stir until the cornstarch is dissolved, then bring the sauce to a rolling boil. Cook for 5 minutes, uncovered.
2 Turn off the heat. Pour in the contents of the 2 cans of canned clams and their juices. Add the chopped fresh herbs and finally, drizzle in the 1/4 tsp of olive oil.
Season with salt, black (or white) pepper, and additional red pepper flakes, if desired.

Variation:
- If you want, you can substitute 1 cup of the water with 1 cup of chicken broth or extra clam juice, for a deeper flavor.
- Add 2 cups of canned, crushed or diced tomatoes and juices in place of 2 cups of water from the base recipe to create Clams and Tomato Sauce, a classic Neapolitan dish.

Sausage Country Gravy

Delicious flavor without the accompanying bypass surgery

This WW-ified country gravy isn't tradition. It's also not prepared by a grumpy line cook, at a truck stop, with a half pound of bacon grease on his apron. This is an incredibly low fat, low calorie version that still has a TON of flavor. Instead of full fat pork sausage, we are using my low fat, healthy, breakfast sausage from page 27. Instead of heavy cream and a mountain of fat, we're going to use almond milk, pan drippings and thickening it all with cornstarch and spices.

Serving Size:
Yields: 5 cups
Servings: (6) 3/4 cup

Points:

	G	B	P
1 serving =	3	1	1
2 servings =	5	2	2
3 servings =	8	4	4
4 servings =	10	5	5

Ingredients:

Breakfast Sausage:
- 1 pound of my 0 point ground turkey breakfast sausage, raw. Recipe on page 27.

"City Boy" Country Gravy
- 4 seconds spray, butter flavored cooking spray
- (or 0 point amount)
- 1-1/2 Tbsp I Can't Believe It's Not Butter Light
- 2 cups unsweetened plain almond milk
- 1 cup water
- 4 Tbsp cornstarch
- 1/2 tsp salt
- 1/2 tsp or more of black pepper, to taste

Directions:

1. Prepare a batch of my ground turkey breakfast sausage ahead of time. Heat a laaaarge pan or a good sized pot, then cook the sausage, using cooking spray.. Break up the meat into small pieces, during cooking.
2. When the meat is cooked through, spray the cooking spray onto the meat, and mix in the butter spread, until melted.
3. In a mixing bowl, combine the almond milk, water and cornstarch until well combined, set aside.
4. Once the pan gets hotter than Ryan Gosling at your front door telling you "Hey girl, let me in... I'm here to vacuum and do your laundry."…. Pour the liquid mixture into the hot pan and start stirring. It should begin to thicken almost immediately.

5. Continue to stir on high heat, allowing the sauce to thicken for another minute or two, until it gets to a nice gravy consistency.
6. Turn off heat and season with salt and pepper, to taste. Don't skimp on the black pepper, because it REALLY makes the sauce taste authentic.

NOTE:
- If you're allergic to almond milk, you can use any similar low point beverage, just adjust your points. Carbmaster brand Lactose free milk at Kroger affiliated stores, is thick, low point, lactose free milk, that has the same thickness as almond milk and is also only 1 point per cup.
- THIS RECIPE IS JUST FOR THE SAUCE!!! You have to make your own biscuits, with whatever recipe you prefer.

Florentine Sauce

A delicously savory cream sauce loaded with fresh spinach

A Florentine Sauce is a savory cream sauce, loaded with fresh spinach, that is typically made with enough heavy cream and butter to give a T1000 a heart attack. This version is based on my Bechamel sauce. That's primarily because it's a great flavorful creamy base... aaaaaand because I'm lazy, so there's that.

Servings:

Yields: 4 cups
Servings: (6) 2/3 cup servings
Points: 1 point per serving

Points:

	G	B	P
1 serving =	1	1	1
2 servings =	2	2	2
3 servings =	3	3	3
4 servings =	4	3	3

Ingredients:

- 1 prepared batch of my Bechamel sauce, recipe pg. 60.
- 3 medium garlic cloves, chopped
- 1 medium onion, diced
- 1/4 cup water**
- 1 tsp chicken flavored bouillon**
- 1 Tbsp white wine
- 1 Tbsp white wine vinegar
- 3 tsp lemon juice
- 4 cups fresh spinach, packed
    (2) 12oz bags of spinach works.
- Butter flavored cooking spray

Directions:

1 Cook the onions and garlic with butter flavored cooking spray for 2-3 minutes on medium heat, until they begin to soften. Add the water, bouillon, wine, vinegar and lemon juirce. Cook till liquid has evaporated.
2 Rough chop the spinach, then add it to the pan. Cover and cook until just starting to wilt.
3 Pour in the prepared Bechamel sauce, stir to combine, then cover pan with lid and bring to a simmer. Cook at a low boil for 3-4 minutes.
4 Season with salt and pepper to taste

Notes:

- Feel free to use frozen spinach if it is more convenient for you. Microwave it, then squeeze out all the liquid.
- You can replace the water and chicken bouillon with 1/4 cup of chicken broth and the sauce will stay 1 point per serving.
- Eating excessive amounts of spinach will **NOT** give you arms like Popeye.
- You can also ladle the sauce onto poached or scrambled eggs, atop an english muffin. It's a snazzy breakfast alternative to Eggs Benedict called Eggs Florentine.

Cook onions, garlic and spinach

Simmer with Bechamel

Use with Chicken, Seafood, and more

It's all Gravy Baby

This is honestly so simple that you're going to facepalm yourself

One of the most frequently requested sauces that I've been asked for that has always puzzled me, because honestly... it's really easy to make, is Gravy. Everyone always says that they miss gravy. I think it's because we're all so used to HAVING to make it 1 certain way, because "that's just how you make it." Get all of the fatty drippings from cooked meat, add a bunch of butter, or cream, or milk, with a garbage can full of flour used to thicken it. Why?!?! There's a really simple formula to make a low point gravy. Heat X amount of liquid, with Y amount of cornstarch, then you end up with Z amount of low point gravy.

Don't have pan drippings? Fine, use canned low sodium broth for your liquid. Don't have canned broth? Fine, use water and beef or chicken granules to make broth. Don't want to use cornstarch? Use Arrowroot. Mix it together, heat it up,... Done. There's a reason why saying that something is "Gravy" is saying that it's easy... it's because it's really easy to make low point.

Ingredients:

- 2 cups of "liquid." It can be pan drippings from meat that's prepared without any oil or butter, canned broth, water with bouillon, or any combination to make 2 cups of "Broth" that's no more than 1 point in total.
- 4 tsp cornstarch
- salt and pepper to taste
  additional herbs or seasonings, as desired.

Directions:

1. Pour the 2 cups of "broth" into a small stock pot (strain the liquid if necessary to remove any solids, if using pan-drippings)
2. Mix the 4 teaspoons of cornstarch with a tiny bit of water to dissolve it. Pour the cornstarch mixture into the broth and stir.
3. Heat the mixture to a boil, then reduce the heat and cook, uncovered, at a low boil for 4-5 minutes.
4. Remove from heat, season with salt and pepper, if needed, then pour into a dish and allow to cool for 5 minutes.

Serving Info.:
Yields: 1-3/4 cups
Servings: 7
Serving Size: 1/4 cup

Points:

	G	B	P
1 serving =	0	0	0
2 servings =	1	1	1
3 servings =	1	1	1
4 servings =	1	1	1

Notes:

- You can substitute Arrowroot for cornstarch as a thickener. It may need to simmer a little longer.
- You can easily double or triple this recipe to make a big ol' barrel of gravy and as long as you follow the formula for liquid to cornstarch ratio, it'll work just fine.
- Remember, if you use drippings from meat cooked with a lot of oil and butter, it will change the points value of the gravy accordingly.
- In my gravy I had 3/4 cup of turkey drippings from my turkey, then added 1 cup chicken broth to get to my 1-3/4 cup.

Hollandaise Sauce

A luxuriously rich and creamy egg yolk and butter sauce

Hollandaise is pretty much the forbidden fruit of sauces when it comes to those of us trying to live a healthy lifestyle. Typically, we save up our points and calories to have the full fat version. The traditional sauce is a very thick, butter and egg yolk sauce, much like a warm mayonnaise. It's perfect over fish, vegetables and even potatoes. The most prized use for Hollandaise is, of course, Eggs Benedict, points be damned!

Luckily for all of your waistlines, I've come up with a way to drastically reduce the points that a GOOD SIZED serving of the sauce comes to. I'm doing this by stretching 6 egg yolks with water, then thickening the mixture with a little cornstarch. Instead of a boat load of butter, we're using a small amount of butter spread and butter flavored cooking spray. We're not barbarians... we're still going to go with white wine vinegar (or lemon juice), whole black peppercorns, bay leaf and a dash of cayenne pepper... I'm crafty, not crazy.

Ingredients:

- 1-1/2 cup water
- 2 Tbsp white wine vinegar *(or lemon juice)*
- 1 Tbsp white wine
- 1-1/2 tsp cornstarch
- 16 whole black peppercorns
- 2 bay leaves
- 2 Tbsp I can't believe it's not butter Light
- 4 second spray, butter flavored cooking spray
- 6 egg yolks (large eggs)
- 1/8 tsp salt
- pinch of paprika or cayenne pepper to garnish

Servings:

Yield: 1-1/2 cups
Servings: 6
Serving Size: 1/4 cup

Points:

	G	B	P
1 serving =	2	1	1
2 servings =	5	1	1
3 servings =	7	2	2
4 servings =	9	2	2

Directions:

1. In a small pot, stir together the water, wine, vinegar (or lemon juice), peppercorns, bay leaves and butter spread. Bring to a rolling boil for 3 minutes. Turn off heat and set aside.
2. Allow mixture to cool for 20 minutes, then strain the liquid.
3. Return strained liquid to the pot, then stir in the cornstarch till dissolved. Whisk in the egg yolks and heat to a low simmer, stirring constantly as soon as the mixture begins to thicken.
4. Continue stirring on low heat, barely simmering for 5-7 minutes.
5. Turn off heat, season with additional salt, if needed.
6. Pour sauce into serving dish or spoon over food. Garnish with a pinch of either paprika or cayenne. Sauce thickens as it cools.

NOTES:

- **BLUE** & **PURPLE** folks, <u>add 2 egg yolks to this sauce</u>, for a total of 8!! I reduced the base recipe to 6 for the **GREEN** folks.
- Everyone has EXTREMELY picky opinion, when it comes to how they like their Hollandaise sauce. This recipe gives you a great low point sauce, so you can add your own tweaks.
- If you want a slightly more "yolk-like" color to your finished sauce, consider adding an 1/8 tsp dash of Turmeric. It will add a earthy hint, but will enhance the color, if that's a big deal to you. Remember, we're stretching 6 egg yolks to 1-1/2 cups.
- The sauce will thicken a little more as it cools due to the cornstarch. If it thickens too much, simply stir in water.
- If you want to a little bit more Fancy Nancy, go ahead and add a little bit of fresh diced shallots to step 1.

10 minute Marinara

This is my really good, though highly controversial, 10 minute Marinara

Let me start off by pointing out the elephant in the room. I KNOW that there are going to be a lot of you that think that you can NOT have an amazing Marinara sauce, without using fancy ingredients, slow simmering a pot o' tomato sauce for 8 hours, all while listening to The Godfather soundtrack. Well, I'm not a Sicilian Grandma with 4 knees, I'm a busy dad with 2 kids and no time. In the past year I've had to streamline my original sauce and come up with a version that can be thrown together, fast... because, well... kids. Ya'know what? It's actually really danged good. It comes together extremely fast, yet is extremely flavorful and is a great base to build off of.

Ingredients:

- 4 second spray, olive oil cooking spray
- 1/4 tsp olive oil
- 4 medium cloves garlic
- 1 small onion, diced
- 1/2 cup chicken broth
- 1 tsp dried basil
- 1 tsp dried oregano
- 1 tsp dried parsley
- 1 Tbsp red wine
- 1 Tbsp red wine vinegar
- 1 to 2 tsp 0 point sweetener o' choice
- 45oz canned tomato sauce
- 1/2 tsp salt
- 1/4 tsp pepper

Yield: 5 cups
Servings: 10
Serving Size: 1/2 cup

Points: (G) (B) (P)

	G	B	P
1 serving =	0	0	0
2 servings =	0	0	0
3 servings =	0	0	0
4 servings =	0	0	0

Directions:

1. Dice the onion and set aside. Chop the garlic and set aside. Put a medium sized pot on your stove and turn the heat up to a medium-high flame, then, get to work. *whip crack*
2. After the pot has had a minute to get nice and hot... Cook the onions for 1-2 minutes, until they start to sweat, then add the garlic, chicken broth, wine, vinegar, dried herbs and sweetener. It will begin bubbling immediately. Allow to cook for 1-2 minutes, or until most of the liquid has dissolved.
3. Pour in the tomato sauce, add the salt and pepper, then bring to a low boil. Pour the sauce into a food processor or blender, or you can use an immersion blender to puree the sauce. Process until the onions are broken down and the sauce is smooth.
4. Season with additional salt and pepper if desired. Done.

Notes:

- You can use sugar instead of artifical sweetener, but you'll need to adjust points accordingly.
- This sauce has no points whatsoever. Feel free to customize it. Add some more olive oil, an extra bit of wine, some additional fresh herbs... whatever you want. This suace is FAST, GOOD, and perfect for using as a base for your own sauce.
- Feel free to get food-snobby and say you haaaaaave to slow simmer marinara for 8 hours, using imported San Marzano tomatoes and 12 year old balsamic. While you're doing that, I'll be over here changing diapers and doing the dishes. 😉 🤣

Mexican Quick Mole

A simplified 'Quick Mole' sauce that can be thrown together in a pinch

Get ready to dodge angry mobs wielding torches and pitchforks because we're about to tackle the most holy of Mexican sauces, Mole' Poblano. Traditionally, Mole' is a very labor intensive sauce that takes an extremely long time to make and includes ingredients like bread, toasted nuts, seeds, peppers, oil, plantains and much more. It usually cooks for hours or even days. This one is ultra fast, flavorful and only 1 points for a 1/2 cup serving.

Serving Size:
Yields: 6 cups
Servings: 12
Serving Size: 1/2 cup servings

Points: Ⓖ Ⓑ Ⓟ
	G	B	P
1 serving =	1	1	1
2 servings =	2	2	2
3 servings =	3	3	3
4 servings =	4	4	4

Ingredients:

- 3-4 medium cloves garlic, chopped
- 29 oz canned tomato sauce
- 1/4 cup 0 point sweetener of choice (monkfruit, stevia, swerve, etc.)
- 3-1/2 Tbsp unsweetened cocoa powder
- 1/2 tsp black pepper
- 3 Tbsp chili powder
- 2 tsp chipotle chili powder (optional but adds nice smokiness)
- 1-1/2 tsp ground cumin
- 1 tsp ground cinnamon
- 2 cups chicken broth, low sodium preferred
- 2 Tbsp PB2 or other brand powdered peanut butter
- 2 Tbsp masa harina (any corn flour will work)
- 1 tsp onion powder
- 2 Tbsp semi-sweet chocolate chips
- 3 tsp sesame seeds, for toasting (toasted sesame seeds are less points)

Directions:

1. Spray a medium sized pot with cooking spray and cook the garlic till just fragrant.
2. Add the tomato sauce, sweetener, cocoa powder, black pepper, chili powder, cumin, cinnamon, broth, powdered peanut butter, masa harina, onion powder and chocolate chips to the pot. Bring to a boil, then lower the heat, cover and simmer for 15-20 mins.
3. Turn off heat and let cool for 30 minutes.
4. Toast the sesame seeds in a small pan over medium heat for 3-4 minutes, till starting to brown, set aside to use as a garnish on your plated meal, 1/4 tsp per serving.

Note:
- In the database, toasted sesame seeds are juuust lower in points than regular. Hence, why we're toasting them for our garnish, rather than using raw sesame seeds.
- At the time of creating this page, the app is bugged. There are only 12 points of ingredients in this recipe on Blue & Purple, yet when you enter this, it shows it as 2 points for the 1st serving. That is WRONG. On Blue & Purple, this sauce has 12 ingredient points and 12 servings.

Pesto Sauce

A fresh, vibrant, savory & versatile green sauce

Pesto is an extremely delicious sauce, primarily consisting of finely processed garlic, tons of basil, different herbs and lots and lots and lots (did I say lots yet?) of olive oil. It is insanely yummie, but insanely high in points. Even popular "skinny" pesto recipes are typically a few points for a small 2 tablespoon serving size. We're upping our game by getting more olive oil flavor with some olive oil cooking spray, minimizing the amount of actual oil, then stretching it with warm water.

Servings:

Yields: 2 cups
Servings: 8
Serving Size: 1/4 cup

Points:

	G	B	P
1 serving =	1	1	1
2 servings =	3	3	3
3 servings =	4	4	4
4 servings =	5	5	5

Ingredients:

- 1 Tbsp pine nuts
- 3-4 medium garlic cloves
- 2 cups basil, stems ok, chopped ***
- 3 cups spinach, packed, chopped ***
- 1/4 cup reduced fat grated parmesan topping (like Kraft brand)
- 1 cup warm water
- 2 tsp lemon juice
- 1 Tbsp olive oil
- 1/2 tsp salt
- 1/4 tsp fresh ground pepper
- olive oil cooking spray, 5 second spray (or 0 point amound, depending on brand)

Directions:

1 Heat a small sauce pan over medium-low heat for 1 minute, then add the pine nuts. Warm the pine nuts for 2-3 minutes, moving them around the pan, till toasted. Set aside.
2 Place all of the ingredients, including the pine nuts, into a food processor or large blender. Spray the olive oil cooking spray for 5 seconds directly onto the ingredients at close range to give them a fair amount of 0 point olive oil flavoring.
3 Process the mixture to break down all of the basil and spinach. Season with additional salt and pepper if desired.

NOTE:

- Basil can be expensive and some folks can't have Spinach, due to dietary restrictions. There are TONS of different greens you can use instead. Experiment with watercress, arugala, kale, collards, mustard greens, even peas. Look online for basil-free Pesto recipes for ideas.
- You can also sub. chopped walnuts in place of the pine nuts. Those babies are expensive too.

Piccata Sauce

Garlic, Lemon and Salty, Briny, Capery Awesomeness

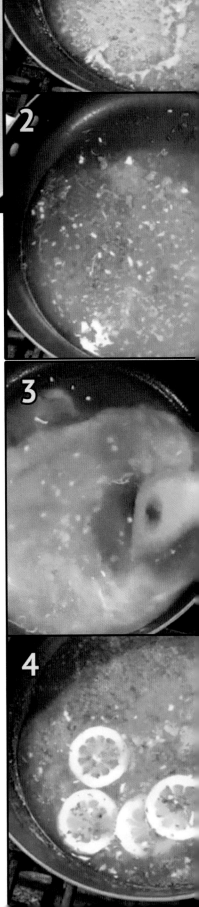

In full disclosure, I understand that most of you reading this are thinking "What the heck is a caper?!" Yes, it COULD be a sneaky plan or bank heist, but it's also a tiny little ball of briny, salty goodness that looks kind of like a tiny sweet pea. I STRONGLY recommend that you buy and cook with **"Non Pareille"** capers. It's written on the jars, it just means those are small capers. Don't use the larger capers, as those are just a big salty jar full of yuck. You can find capers in the grocery store by the olives and vinegars typically.

Ingredients:

- 2-3 cloves garlic, chopped
- 5 second spray, butter flavored cooking spray
- 3/4 cup water
- 3/4 cup chicken broth
- 3 Tbsp lemon juice
- 1-1/2 tsp cornstarch
- 1/4 tsp olive oil
- 1 Tbsp I Can't Believe It's Not Butter Light**
- 2 Tbsp capers
- 1 tsp dried parsley flakes
- Salt and pepper to taste
- Thin lemon slices for garnish
- Fresh chopped parsley for garnish

Serving Info.:

Yields: 1-1/2 cups
Servings: 4
Serving Size: 1/3 cup

Points:

	G	B	P
1 serving =	1	1	1
2 servings =	1	1	1
3 servings =	2	1	1
4 servings =	2	1	1

Directions:

1 Sweat the garlic in a medium pan with cooking spray, until it becomes fragrant. Add the water, broth, lemon juice, cornstarch, olive oil and butter spread. Stir to combine, heat to a rolling boil.
2 Stir in the capers and parsley flakes and simmer for 2-3 minutes.
3 Once the sauce begins to cling to your spoon, add a few thin lemon slices and stir around in the sauce.
4 It should take around 1 minute for the lemons to begin to soften and break down. Turn off the heat, season with salt and pepper to taste, then spoon the finished sauce over your meat.

Note:

- For best results, add your cooked meat to the pan and allow to simmer in the sauce for a minute, turning to coat.
- As with everything I make, this sauce is tasty as-is, however it's so low in points and calories that you have plenty of room to add some more butter spread or olive oil.

Red Enchilada Sauce

This is a very fast, low fat and simple take on a Mexican classic

I need to start by addressing all of my Latino amigos that are reading this page. I understand that I've already messed with your Mole' sauce, I've already had you put fat free yogurt into Masa to make 3 point Gringo Tamales on Connect (#dhallakvids), I know that right now you're probably waving your fists in the sky and yelling "what more could this guy do to us?!" Well sorry, but I'm messing with your enchilada sauce now. Traditionally, red enchilada sauce is an incredibly delicious and spicy (depending on the peppers you use) puree of water, seasonings, a BOAT LOAD of oil and tons and tons and tons of dried hot chili peppers. In order to make it really low in points, we need to eliminate the oil. That's why I decided to replace it with tomato sauce and regular chili powder from the spice aisle. The reason being that it is more readily available to people and the thought of dealing with a big bag of dried chili peppers is an intimidating turn off to a lot of folks.

Ingredients:

- 2-1/2 cups water
- 1 tsp chicken flavored bouillon powder/granules
  (OR replace 1/2 cup of the water with 1/2 cup of chicken broth)
- 4 Tbsp california, chipotle, or anaheim chili powder***
  (can use a different type of ground chili if desired)
- 1 Tbsp chili powder *(regular generic chili powder)*
- 1-1/2 tsp garlic powder
- 1-1/2 tsp onion powder
- 1-1/2 tsp ground cumin
- 1/4 tsp salt
- 30 oz canned tomato sauce *(0 point tomato sauce)*

Directions:

1 Pour ALL of the ingredients into a medium sized pot and stir to combine over medium heat.
2 Bring the sauce to a boil, then cover and reduce the heat to a low simmer. Allow sauce to simmer covered for 15 minutes, stirring occasionally.
3 Remove from heat and season to taste.

Serving Size:

Yields: 6 cups
Servings: 12
Serving Size: 1/2 cup

Points:**

	G	B	P
1 serving =	0	0	0
2 servings =	1	1	1
3 servings =	1	1	1
4 servings =	1	1	1

NOTES:

- Various types of dried chili powders can be found in the spice aisle (McCormick's sells chipotle chili powder), or usually in the Latin section of most supermarkets.
- Add actual pureed chilis or hot sauce if you want, to add more 0 point heat.
- Pairing this sauce with 1 point tortillas or wraps, shredded chicken, veggies, and the Fat Free cheese hack will give you some extreeemely legit, low point enchiladas.
- This sauce goes really well with my 3 point Tamales. You can find them in Connect under #dhallaktamales, or on my youtube channel "The Guilt Free Gourmet."
- This is another one of those recipes that is wonky in the recipe builder. It has only 4 ingredient points, spread across 12 servings. When entered into the builder, it shows the first serving as 1 point. It's SUPPOSED to be 0. Scroll the servings from 1, to 0, then back to 1... and the points magically change to the correct value. Pull up this same recipe on the GREEN plan?.... 4 points, 12 servings, 1st serving is 0. Switch to Blue or Purple? 1st serving is 1sp, unless you do the scroll back to 0 servings, then back to 1 serving trick. If your recipe builder is acting like a poopyhead, try the scroll down then back up trick. It resets it to the correct points.

Roasted Red Pepper Marinara

A mildly sweet marinara-style sauce made with roasted red peppers

This sauce is proof that it may take me a long time to get to a recipe, but eventually I'll get around to it. About 5 months ago, I promised **@dtspilde** on Connect that I'd make a marinara sauce that doesn't have any tomato in it because of food allergies. After a little searching online, I found that making marinara sauce with Roasted Red Peppers is a great way to do it. The addition of red wine, chicken broth and the sauteed carrots and red onion also help give it more depth.

Ingredients:

- 5 large red bell peppers, chopped
- 5 medium cloves fresh garlic
- olive oil cooking spray
- 1 large red onion, rough chopped
- 1-1/2 cups chopped carrots
- 1 tsp italian seasoning
- 1/2 tsp garlic powder
- 1/2 tsp onion powder
- 1/2 tsp dried basil
- 1/2 tsp dried thyme
- 1 Tbsp I Can't Believe It's Not Butter Light
- 1-1/2 cups chicken broth
- 1/2 cup chicken or vegetable broth
- 2 tsp red wine vinegar
- 2 Tbsp red wine

Serving Info.:

Yields: 5 cups
Serving Size: 1/2 cup
Servings: 10

Points:

	G	B	P
1 serving =	0	0	0
2 servings =	0	0	0
3 servings =	1	1	1
4 servings =	1	1	1

Note:

- If you don't want to use red wine in your sauce, you can replace it with 2 Tbsp of Balsamic Vinegar for the same amount of points.
- If you're allergic to tomatoes, but can have bell peppers... use this as a tomato sauce replacement in recipes, but adjust seasonings.

Directions:

1 Preheat your oven to 425 degrees and line a sheet pan with aluminum foil,
2 Cut the red peppers into large pieces, remove the seeds and arrange on the sheet pan along with the fresh cloves of garlic. Coat with olive oil cooking spray, make sure it's a 0 point amount of spray. Season lightly with salt and pepper, then bake at 425 for 20-25 minutes. Remove when the peppers are cooked through and pliable.
3 Spray a large saucepan with cooking spray and saute' the red onion and carrots for 2-3 minutes on medium-high heat. Add the butter spread and stir till it melts. Add the italian seasoning, garlic powder, onion powder, dried basil, thyme, broth, vinegar, chicken broth and red wine. Bring to a boil and allow to simmer for 3-4 minutes.
4 Pour the contents of the sauce pan into a food processor or large blender, along with all of the roasted garlic and red bell peppers. Peeling the skins from the peppers is optional.
5 Puree on high speed for a minimum of 1 minute or until the sauce is smooth, adding more broth, if desired, to thin the sauce more. Season with salt and pepper, to taste.

Roasted Tomatillo Sauce

A deliciously fresh and flavorful traditional Mexican green sauce

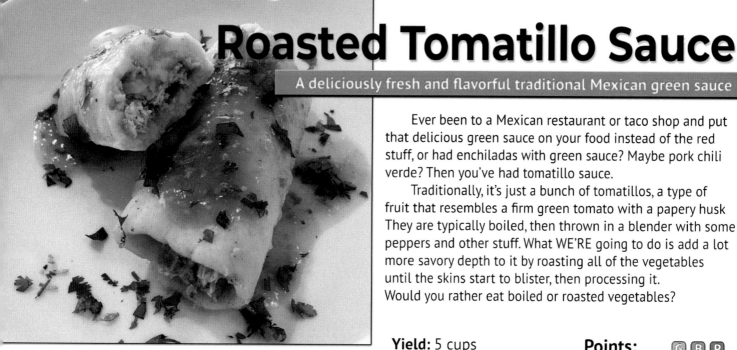

3 point chicken tamales with roasted tomatillo sauce

Ever been to a Mexican restaurant or taco shop and put that delicious green sauce on your food instead of the red stuff, or had enchiladas with green sauce? Maybe pork chili verde? Then you've had tomatillo sauce.

Traditionally, it's just a bunch of tomatillos, a type of fruit that resembles a firm green tomato with a papery husk They are typically boiled, then thrown in a blender with some peppers and other stuff. What WE'RE going to do is add a lot more savory depth to it by roasting all of the vegetables until the skins start to blister, then processing it. Would you rather eat boiled or roasted vegetables?

Yield: 5 cups
Servings: 10 servings
Serving Size: 1/2 cup
Points: 0 points per serving

Points:

	G	B	P
1 serving =	0	0	0
2 servings =	0	0	0
3 servings =	0	0	0
4 servings =	0	0	0

Ingredients:

- 2-1/2 lbs. Tomatillos, husks and stems removed
- 1 medium onion, rough chopped
- 2 medium green bell peppers, rough chopped, seeds removed
- 3 medium cloves garlic
- 4 good sized Pasilla peppers, chopped, seeds removed (they aren't spicy)
- 1/2 bunch fresh cilantro, around 1 handful
- 1/2 tsp salt
- 1 whole Jalapeno pepper *(OPTIONAL!)*

Notes:

- Tomatillos are very easy to clean for this sauce, just pull the husks back like the husks on an ear of corn, twist the stem and pull. Remove any dirt or debris and you're good to go.
- Tomatillos have a sticky feel to them, that's fine.
- Add the Jalapeno to the roasting pan, if you want a spicy sauce. This base recipe is for a completely mild and non spicy sauce.
- If you plan to use this sauce for enchiladas, add some water or chicken broth to thin it out a bit.
- This sauce is delicious served with tacos, tamales, over chicken, pork, on nachos, enchiladas, eggs, pretty much anything.

Directions:

1. Preheat your oven to 375 degrees.
2. Line a large sheet pan with foil and spray with olive oil cooking spray.
3. Place all of the vegetables on the tray and spray them liberally with the cooking spray, then sprinkle lightly with salt and pepper.
4. Cook the vegetables at 375 degrees for 45 minutes, or until the tops of the vegetables are starting to blacken.
5. Turn the broiler to high in your oven and place the tray on the top rack under the broiler. Watch so that the vegetables don't burn to a crisp. You want to develop some black char across the tops of some of them.
6. Remove the tray from the oven and spoon all of the roasted veggies into a food processor or large blender. Make sure to also pour all of the juices in as well, along with the fresh cilantro and 1/4 tsp salt.
7. Process the vegetables on high for up to 1 minute. It should give you a thick green salsa.

Scampi Sauce

A spicy, lemon butter, white wine, garlic, herb sauce

Scampi sauce is a delicious, zesty, herbed lemon garlic sauce that goes fantastic with all types of seafood and poultry. It's most popular application is, of course, Shrimp Scampi. In this recipe I'll be adding Shrimp into the ingredients, even though this is really supposed to be a recipe page for just the sauce. I'm including how to actually use it to make a dish,.. why not, it's my book after all.

Ingredients:

- 4 medium cloves garlic, chopped
- 5 second spray, butter flavored cooking spray
- 1-1/2 cup chicken broth
- 3 Tbsp white wine
- 2 Tbsp white wine vinegar
- 3 tsp cornstarch, dissolved in a little water
- 2 Tbsp I can't believe it's not butter Light
- 2 Tbsp lemon juice
- 1/4 tsp salt
- 1/8 tsp black pepper
- 1/8 - 1/4 tsp red pepper flakes to taste *(OPTIONAL)*
- 1 Tbsp fresh parsley, finely chopped
- 2 Tbsp fresh oregano, finely chopped

Servings:

Yields: 1-3/4 cup sauce
Servings: 7
Servin Size: 1/4 cup sauce

Points:

	G	B	P
1 serving =	1	1	1
2 servings =	1	1	1
3 servings =	2	2	2
4 servings =	3	3	3

Directions:

1. Spray a medium saucepan for 5 seconds with olive oil cooking spray, then saute garlic over medium heat till fragrant.

2. Add the broth, wine, vinegar, cornstarch, butter spread, lemon juice, salt, and pepper to the pan. Bring to a rolling boil for 3 minutes, allowing the sauce to start thickening.

3. Add red pepper flakes, parsley and oregano to the pan, continue cooking at a low simmer for an additional 2 minutes, or until the sauce coats the back of a spoon. Done.

4. Additionally, if you want to make a traditional shrimp or chicken scampi dish, now would be the time when you'd add your raw shrimp or diced raw chicken to the simmering sauce. If cooking shrimp, place the shrimp into the simmering scampi sauce and toss to coat. Cook for 2 minutes or until the shrimp is a light pink color throughout. Cook chicken slightly longer, till cooked through.

Vodka Sauce

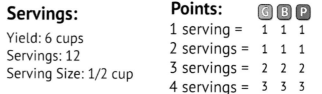

This sauce was a direct result of a post that I saw trending in Connect, from member *@libra.1019,* saying how much she missed pasta with Vodka sauce, and that the advice she received at her workshop was more focussed on "eat the regular full fat version, but a smaller portion, this is a lifestyle", which I call BS on. Why have a small, unsatisfying fatty micro meal, when you can have a healthy, regular sized version that's lower in calories, fat and points than the sad little tiny plate? So... here we are. This Vodka sauce is a modern take on a classic tomato sauce. Infused with lots sauteed onions, garlic, fresh basil, black pepper, balsamic, spicy red pepper flakes, VODKA and "cream", this sauce is simple to make, but has a complex depth.

Ingredients:

- 4 medium cloves fresh garlic, rough chopped
- 1 medium onion, diced
- 1 tsp salt
- 1/4 tsp black pepper
- 1/4 tsp red pepper flakes
- olive oil cooking spray, 8 second spray
- (1) 29oz canned crushed tomatoes.
- (1) 15oz canned crushed tomatoes
- 1/4 cup Vodka PLUS 1 tablespoon water *(1/3 cup total)*
- 1/2 cup fresh basil, chopped
- 2 tsp balsamic vinegar
- 1 tsp red wine vinegar
- 1 cup unsweetened plain almond milk
- 2 Tbsp reduced fat Parmesan-Style grated topping
  (like the Kraft sprinkles you get at a pizzaria, in a shaker)

Servings:

Yield: 6 cups
Servings: 12
Serving Size: 1/2 cup

Points: Ⓖ Ⓑ Ⓟ

	G	B	P
1 serving =	1	1	1
2 servings =	1	1	1
3 servings =	2	2	2
4 servings =	3	3	3

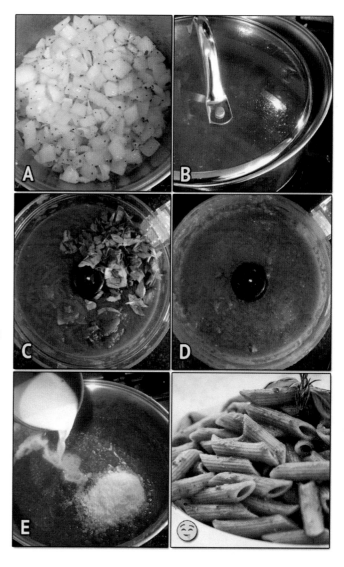

Directions:

1. In a medium sized pot, spray the cooking spray over the onions, garlic, salt, pepper and red pepper flakes. Cook until softened, around 6-7 minutes on medium heat.
2. Add the crushed tomatoes, vodka mixture, and vinegars. Cover and allow to cook at a low simmer for 20 minutes.
3. Carefully pour the hot sauce into a food processor, with the fresh chopped basil, then puree until almost smooth. You can also use a blender, in batches.
4. Return the sauce to your pot, add parmesan topping and almond milk. Stir to combine, then cover and simmer for 5 minutes. Done

Notes:

- Big bottles of Vodka are expensive. They sell small $3 bottles at corner liquor stores or at BevMo, any brand works.
- If you can't use almond milk, due to allergies, use soy or cashew milk. Kroger also has an awesome brand of low point, thick milk, called "Carbmaster" that's 1 point per cup. Honestly though, this is so low in points, with so many servings, that you can use whatever you want. Just remember to adjust the points.

White Wine Butter & Garlic Sauce

A delicious herbed garlic butter sauce with a subtle wine taste

Servings Info.:
- Yields: 2 cups
- Servings: 8
- Serving Size: 1/4 cup

Points:

	G	B	P
1 serving =	1	1	1
2 servings =	1	1	1
3 servings =	2	2	2
4 servings =	2	2	2

You would be a straight up liar if you said that you didn't love a good white wine butter sauce, but let's see... what's the main problem with that sauce if you're in Weight Watchers? Oh yeah, a giganto amount of points from butter and wine. Here's the deal though, simply follow the ideas in this guide and figure out how to OUT SMART your food. A few simple food swaps, from thinking outside of the box, makes this sauce possible. We up the servings by stretching with water and chicken broth, to lower the points per serving. Ask yourself, do we REALLY need 1/2 cup of white wine in the sauce? Guess what, 3 Tbsp of it, plus 2 Tbsp of white wine vinegar will still give a great wine flavor, just a more subtle one. Do we really need a ton of butter? Nope. Let's use I Can't Believe It's Not Butter Light, along with some butter flavored cooking spray, to impart a buttery flavor at a fraction of the points. But how do we thicken it without a bunch of heavy cream?... Cornstarch. It'll tighten it up for 40 calories and no fat.

Ingredients:
- 4 second spray, butter flavored cooking spray
- 1 cup chicken broth
- 3/4 cup water
- 3 Tbsp white wine
- 2 Tbsp white wine vinegar
- 1-1/2 Tbsp I can't believe it's not butter Light
- 1 medium garlic clove, chopped
- 1 tsp dried parsley or basil
- 4-1/2 tsp cornstarch
- 1/4 tsp salt
- 1/8 tsp pepper

Directions:
1. Combine all of the ingredients in a small sauce pot, whisk to combine.
2. Bring the sauce to a rolling boil over, high heat.
3. Allow the sauce to cook at a rolling boil for 4 minutes.
4. Remove from heat and season with salt and pepper, to taste. It will thicken more as it cools.

Notes:
- If you would like a creamier sauce for no additional points, you can replace 1/4 cup of the water with 1/4 cup of unsweetened almond milk. You can also use 3 Tbsp of fat free/skim milk in place of an equal amount of the water.
- You can add in some red pepper flakes, different herbs than parsley, and some lemon juice, but then you'd be treading on the "Scampi Sauce" recipe's territory.
- This same principle can be used to make a red wine sauce. Replace the chicken broth with beef broth, the white wine with red, use red wine vinegar, remove the parsley and basil, then increase the salt to 1/2 tsp and the black pepper to 1/4 tsp.

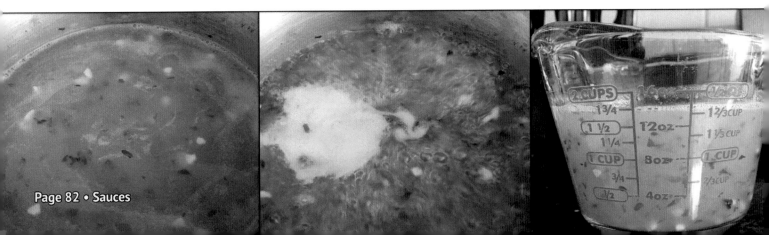

Hummus

Traditionally, Hummus is made with garbanzo beans, garlic, lemon juice, tahini (crushed sesame seed paste), and lots and lots and loooooooooots of extra virgin olive oil. It's usually so high in points and calories that the popular skinny cooking sites, and even the manufacturers, have their serving sizes at a mere 2 tablespoons. Anyone who has ever had hummus knows... 2 Tablespoons is NOT a realistic serving size. I also decided to do an even lower point, GREEN PLAN friendly version, because Garbanzo beans have points on Green, which bumped up the points of the first serving. I am absolutely determined to keep the first serving at 1 point, so I had to hack my own recipe. I removed the 2 Tbsp of tahini, which is just ground up sesame seed paste, and replaced it with some extra sesame oil and a few teaspoons of powdered peant butter. Boom.

LOW POINT HUMMUS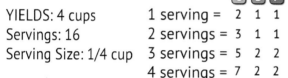

	G	B	P
YIELDS: 4 cups			
Servings: 16			
Serving Size: 1/4 cup			
1 serving =	2	1	1
2 servings =	3	1	1
3 servings =	5	2	2
4 servings =	7	2	2

Ingredients:

- (2) 15oz cans of garbanzo beans/chickpeas, drained, reserve liquid. You are left with 17.5oz of drained chickpeas.
- 2 Tbsp tahini (sesame paste)
- 1/4 cup lemon juice
- 3-4 fresh garlic cloves (to taste)
- 2 Tbsp reserved garbanzo bean juice
- 3 Tbsp water
- 1/3 cup fat free yogurt (or greek)
- 1 tsp extra virgin olive oil
- 2 tsp ground cumin
- 1 tsp salt
- 1/4 tsp sesame oil *(OPTIONAL, though RECOMMENDED!!)*

Directions:

1 Drain the garbanzo beans, reserve the liquid, and rinse off the beans.
2 Add the garbanzo beans, tahini, lemon juice, garlic, garbanzo bean juice, water, yogurt, oils, cumin, and salt to a large blender or food processor and process until pureed and smooth.
3 If the mixture is too thick, add more reserved garbanzo bean juice, 1 Tablespoon at a time, until it takes on a very smooth, creamy, and easily spreadable consistency. Season with more salt and pepper, if necessary.
4 Garnish with a dusting of paprika and minced parsley. Spray the top of the hummus with a quick touch of olive oil cooking spray.

GREEN PROGRAM HUMMUS

	G	B	P
YIELDS: 4 cups			
Servings: 16			
Serving Size: 1/4 cup			
1 serving =	1	0	0
2 servings =	3	0	0
3 servings =	4	1	1
4 servings =	5	1	1

Ingredients:

- (2) 15oz cans of garbanzo beans/chickpeas, drained, reserve liquid. You are left with 17.5oz of drained chickpeas.
- 1/4 tsp olive oil
- 1-1/2 tsp sesame oil (strong sesame flavor, replaces the tahini)
- 1/3 cup plain fat free Greek yogurt
- 5 Tbsp reserved chickpea juice
- 1/4 cup lemon juice
- 2 tsp ground cumin
- 1 tsp salt
- 3-4 medium cloves garlic (start with 3, puree, then taste)
- 3-1/2 tsp powdered peanut butter (PB2)

Directions:

1 Add ALL of the ingredients into a food processor and puree on high for 1-2 minutes, or until mixture is completely smooth and creamy. Add a little bit more almond milk, if necessary.

NOTES:

- In this recipe, we're lowering the points a bit, by removing the tahini and replacing it with a bit more sesame oil instead. Tahini is ground up sesame seed paste, imagine it kind of like thinner peanut butter that's made out of sesame seeds rather than peanuts. 2 Tbsp of tahini is a good deal of points. Here, we're taking all of those points away and instead we're using more potent and much lower in point, sesame seed oil. To give the slight nutty flavor, we're adding a 0 point amount of powdered peanut butter. Doing that, allows us to get the first 1/4 cup down to 1 point for Green folks.

Holiday Dishes

Considering that this guide is coming out right around Thanksgiving & Christmas, everyone is probably stressing out, trying to figure out how to do low point & calorie, WW-Friendly side dishes... that their family will actually eat.

I figured I'd deliver an early Christmas present to everyone, so I'm tacking on a few really good, really low point and really low calorie and fat recipes for traditional holiday side dishes... but done MY way.

In the original Guide that came out in 2018, I included a few side dishes. This time, I'm going to also include an appetizer and an AWESOME Fall dessert, a delicious and snazzy Pumpkin Pie Spice cake. Might as well help cover all the bases.

Appetizer:
Sausage Stuffed Mushrooms ... pg 86-87

Sides:
Chicken Divan ... pg 88-89
Green Bean Casserole ... pg 90-91
Low Point Gravy ... pg 71
(in the sauces section)
Stuffing/Dressing ... pg 92-93
Sweet Potato Casserole ... pg 94-95
Corn Muffins ... pg 96
Spiced Cranberry Sauce ... pg 97

Dessert:
Pumpkin Spice Cake ... pg 98-99

Bonus Dish:
Low Point & Calorie Tamales ... pg 100-101

Stuffed Mushrooms

Italian Sausage Stuffed Mushrooms with Herbed "Cream Cheese"

This is my WW-erized, lower fat, calorie and point version of Ina Garten's famous sausage stuffed mushrooms. I used my 0 point Italian sausage in place of regular, swapped mascarpone for strained Greek yogurt, then used crushed rice crispies instead of breadcrumbs. Adios fat and calories!

Servings Info.:
Yield: 38 mushrooms**
Servings: 38**
Serving Size: 1 mushroom

Points:

	G	B	P
1 serving =	0	0	0
2-3 servings =	1	0	0
4-6 servings =	2	1	1
7-8 servings =	3	1	1

Blue & Purple can have up to 11 servings for 1 point

Ingredients:

- (2) 24oz cartons, medium sized whole mushrooms. I used Cremini mushrooms, but you can use any variety, as long as they are "Legal" mushrooms. I'm lookin at you *@kingdayvid*!

Filling Mixture:
- *1 pound of my 0 point Italian Sausage*
  (Recipe in the Foundation section)
- 1/2 cup diced onion
- 3 medium cloves garlic, minced
- 2 cups finely diced mushroom stems
- 1/2 tsp salt
- 2 tsp worcestershire sauce
- 1/2 cup chopped fresh basil (added at the end)

"Bread Crumbs": (makes about 2/3 cup total)
- 1-1/4 cups rice krispies cereal, crushed. *(makes around 1/2 cup)*
- 1-1/2 tsp plain breadcrumbs
- 2 tsp panko breadcrumbs
- 1/4 tsp black pepper
- 1/2 tsp italian seasoning
- 1/2 tsp dried basil
- 1/2 tsp onion powder
- 1/2 tsp garlic powder

"Cream Cheese Substitute":
- *1 cup plain fat free Greek Yogurt (I use Fage for this)*
- *1/2 tsp garlic powder*
- *1/2 tsp onion powder*
- *1 tsp italian seasoning*
- *1/4 tsp salt*
- *Paper Coffee Filters or Cheese Cloth, with a strainer*

Garnish:
- *2 tsp reduced fat grated parmesan topping (like Kraft)*
- *Additional chopped fresh basil (or italian parsley)*

Directions:

1. This needs to be done first, start it the night before. Let's make cream cheese substitute, boys and girls! Line a strainer with either cheese cloth or paper coffee filters. Scoop the Greek yogurt into the strainer, place over a bowl and cover with plastic wrap. Allow it to sit overnight. I highly recommend Fage brand for this.

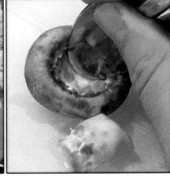

2. YOU NEED TO CLEAN THE MUSHROOMS!!! Out of the package, they have dirt and yuck all over them. So, get 1 mushroom lightly wet at your sink, then gently scrub it with a kitchen brush. Gently pull off the stem, then use a small spoon to clean out a cavity for your filling. Save the stem in a bowl for later. Cover a large pan or plate with paper towels, then place the mushroom cap onto the paper towel, cavity facing down. Repeat with every mushroom till all are cleaned.

3. **(A)** Finely dice 2 cups of mushroom stems, set aside.
(B) Add the italian sausage to a large pan, along with the onion and garlic. Cook over med-high heat until browned.
(C) Add diced mushroom stems and cook for 3-4 minutes.
(D) Stir in the crushed rice krispies "breading" and fresh chopped basil. Use a spoon to combine. Turn off the heat.

4. **(A)** Remove Greek yogurt from the fridge, scoop into a bowl and mix in the onion and garlic powders, italian seasoning and salt. **(B)** With the heat turned off, mix the yogurt, along with 2 teaspoons of worcestershire sauce, into the filling.
(C) The finished mixture should be thick and hold together.
(D) Using measuring spoons, scoop 1 even tablespoon into the large mushrooms and fill the smaller mushroom with less filling. Don't go over 1 tablespoon per mushroom though. The sizes of the 'shrooms vary, so your exact number of servings will vary, per batch. I made 38 before I ran out of filling.

5. **(A)** Line a baking pan with tin foil, then spray with cooking spray. Place the mushrooms tightly together on the pan, then spray the tops with cooking spray and lightly sprinkle 1 teaspoon of grated parmesan on top of the mushrooms.
(B) Bake for 20-24 minutes at 375 degrees. **(C)** There will be a good deal of liquid at the bottom of the pan, so when you remove the pan from the oven, set one corner of the pan on a kitchen spoon or dish towel, to raise it up, and draw all of the liquid to one corner. **(D)** Use a slotted spoon to place each of the mushrooms onto a platter, allowing more of the liquid to run off. Garnish with fresh chopped basil and the rest of the parmesan cheese topping.

NOTES:

A) These can be fully assembled onto your sheet pan, up to 1 day before baking, WHICH IS AWESOME! Place all of the assembled mushrooms on your baking pan, like in step (5a), then wrap the entire pan in plastic wrap and store in the fridge, until ready to bake.

Chicken Divan Casserole

Diced chicken breast, broccoli and onions, in a creamy and savory cheese sauce

Chicken Divan is my absolute favorite thing to eat at Thanksgiving, it reminds me of my mom. She used to make it every year, it was my favorite dish and I always looked forward to it. After she died, I didn't have it for around 10 years. When I started WW, I told myself that if I ever lost my first 20 pounds... making a WW-ified version would be my reward. I figured that would take months, It took 3-4 weeks. I never found my mom's recipe, so I used Paula Dean's. Hers came to 20 points PER SERVING and had enough fat to send Godzilla into cardiac arrest. This version is freaking awesome, comes together fast and is great as a side dish or as a main dish. If you don't want to use Fat Free cheese, I include notes for what the points would change to, using reduced fat cheese.

Servings Info.:

Yield: 11 cups
Servings: 11
Serving Size: 1 cup

Points:

	G	B	P
1 serving =	3	2	2
2 servings =	6	3	3
3 servings =	9	4	4

(increases 1 point when using reduced fat cheese, instead of fat free)

Ingredients:

- 2-1/2 pounds fresh broccoli, around 3 large heads. Florets trimmed, stems cut into chunks.
- 1 large onion, diced
- 2 medium cloves garlic, chopped
- 1-1/2 pounds diced chicken breast
- 1/2 tsp celery salt
- 1/4 tsp pepper
- 1/2 tsp onion powder

Cheese Sauce:
- 1 (11oz) can Campbells "Heart Healthy" condensed cheddar cheese soup (lower calorie and points than regular)
- 1/2 cup chicken broth
- 1/4 tsp turmeric
- 1 tsp paprika
- 1/2 tsp onion powder
- 1/2 tsp salt
- 1/4 tsp pepper
- 1 Tbsp white wine
- 1 Tbsp white wine vinegar
- 1 Tbsp cornstarch, dissolved with 1 Tbsp water
- 1 cup Fat Free shredded cheddar cheese (at walmart)**
- 3/4 cup Fat Free shredded mozzarella (at walmart)**
- 1 cup fat free plain Greek yogurt

Topping:
- 1 cup Rice Krispies cereal
- 0 point Butter flavored cooking spray**

Directions:

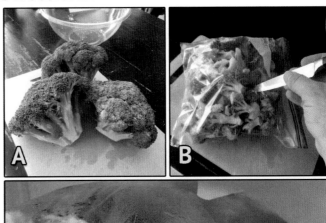

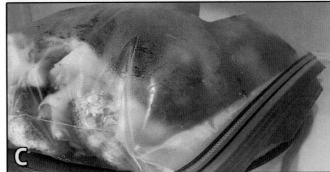

1. **(A)** Take your fresh broccoli heads, then trim off the florets and place in a bowl. Chop the stems, then place all of the broccoli into a gallon sized ziplock bag. **(B)** Add 2 Tablespoons of water into the bag, then zip the bag closed. Poke 2 holes into the bag to vent. **(C)** Place the bag into your microwave, and heat for 3 minutes. Remove bag from the microwave and set aside, leaving the bag closed.

3. **(A)** Add the canned soup, broth, turmeric, paprika, onion powder, salt, pepper, white wine, vinegar, and dissolved cornstarch to a sauce pan. **(B)** Stir over medium/high heat until thick and creamy. Turn off heat. **(C)** Add the cheeses and yogurt, then **(D)** stir until it's thick, cheesy goop.

4. Preheat over to 375 degrees. **(A)** In a laaaaaarge mixing bowl, combine the broccoli, chicken, onion and cheese sauce until well mixed, then pour into a 13 x 9 casserole dish *(I used a large 4.5qt one)*. **(B)** Measure 1 cup of Rice Krispies, then crush in a ziplock bag. Add to a small bowl, then spray for a few seconds (0 points worth) of butter flavored cooking spray onto the crushed cereal. Mix together with a fork till crumbly. Spread the "buttered" crumbs over the top of the casserole. **(C)** Place the casserole onto the 2nd from the top rack of the oven. Bake at 375 for 45 minutes. **(D)** If you want your crust more golden, turn on your broiler for 2-3 minutes. Keep an eye on it so that it doesn't burn. Done.

NOTES:

A) Don't want to use Fat Free shredded cheese? Not a problem. You can use reduced fat cheese, though it will increase the points to 3 points for 1 serving.

B) **Butter Flavored Cooking spray. The amount of spray that you can use, depends on the brand that you use. Some brands let you have 6-8 seconds of spray for 0 points, while others let you spray coat a '67 Buick for 2 points. Scan your can and adjust your usage accordingly.

C) If you're not used to using your oven's broiler, watch it carefully. Your topping can go from golden to burned, fast.

2. **(A)** Use canola or olive oil cooking spray to saute the onions and garlic until softened, about 5 minutes. Set aside. **(B)** Season chicken with celery salt, onion powder and pepper, cook until just cooked through. Remove from heat and set aside.

Green Bean Casserole

Green bean casserole is a holiday staple that's usually pretty high in points. We're making it lower in points by adding mushrooms and onions to stretch out the number of servings, which will decrease the points per serving. We're also using reduced fat grated parmesan as a low point tasty binder.

Ingredients:

- 1 large onion, chopped
- 3 cloves fresh garlic, chopped
- 16 oz. fresh sliced mushrooms
- 1/2 cup chicken broth
- 2 tsp worcestershire sauce
- 1 tsp onion powder
- 1/2 tsp garlic powder
- 2 (10.5 oz) cans reduced fat/sodium condensed cream of mushroom soup (see note)**
- 3 tsp cornstarch, dissolved in a little water
- 9 cups frozen cut green beans, thawed (*3 12 oz bags*)**
- 1/4 cup grated parmesan topping, reduced fat *(Kraft)*
- 1 cup French's crispy fried onions, crushed and packed
- salt and pepper to taste

Servings Info.:

Yield: 7 cups
Servings: 13
Serving Size: 2/3 cup

Points: G B P

	G	B	P
1 serving =	2	2	2
2 servings =	4	4	4
3 servings =	6	6	6

Directions:

1. Preheat oven to 350 degrees, then spray a large pan with cooking spray and cook onions and garlic on medium heat, 4-5 minutes until softened.

2. Add chicken broth, worcestershire, onion powder and garlic powder to the pan, cover and cook for 5 minutes at a low simmer.

3. Add the sliced mushrooms to the pan, cover, and cook for 5 minutes over medium heat.

4. Stir in the 2 cans of cream of mushroom soup and dissolved cornstarch. Stir until well combined and contents of the pan are coated.

5. Cook at a low simmer uncovered for 5 minutes, stirring occasionally. Season with salt and pepper.

6. Remove pan from heat. Add all of the green beans to the pan and gently fold to combine. Coat all of the beans with the sauce. Return to heat until just heated through.

7. Once the sauce has started to bubble, turn off the heat and stir in the grated parmesan cheese and 1/4 cup of crushed French's fried onions.

8. Pour the contents of the pan into a 3 quart casserole dish. Bake for 40 minutes at 350.

9. Remove pan from oven and sprinkle top of the casserole with 3/4 cups of crushed French's fried onions. Return the casserole to the oven, turn the oven temperature up to 375 degrees and cook for an additional 10-15 minutes.

10. Allow the casserole to cool uncovered for 10 minutes before serving. Sauce thickens more as it cools.

NOTES:

A) You can use fresh cut green beans instead of the frozen ones, in which case I would recommend either boiling them in water for a few minutes to soften them a little bit and then rinse them under cold water to stop the cooking process, or sautee them covered for 4-5 minutes and then remove from heat and set aside. Then follow the directions as normal.

B) If you don't want to use mushrooms, you can replace them with more green beans. You need to make up the bulk of the removed mushrooms with something else to keep the same number of servings and points.

C) You can replace the low fat/sodium condensed cream of mushroom soup, with cream of chicken soup if you don't like mushrooms.

D) If your sauce is TOO thick at the end of step 5, stir in a little bit more chicken broth to thin it.

E) Don't forget to taste the sauce prior to mixing in the green beans so that you can add more seasoning, if needed.

F) One of the BIGGEST things that you might be trying to figure out is the how I came up with 9 points for 2 (10.5 oz) cans of reduced fat/sodium cream of mushroom soup, rather than the 12 points that the WW app would lead you to think it is. Well, allow me to explain, because the actual soup can is wrong in this case. The CAN of soup says that 1 serving size is 1/2 cup and that there is 2.5 servings (1.25 cups per can). HOWEVER.... the can is wrong. If you actually pour the contents of the can out and measure them there is exactly 1 cup of condensed soup per can, not 1-1/4 cups like the can's listed servings (and points) suggest.

If you enter the nutritional info for the can into the app with 2 servings (1 cup) rather than 2.5 servings (1.25 cups), it gives a point value of 4 points for 1 cup (the real contents of the can, not 1.25 cups). The contents of 2 cans of soup, which is 2 cups, is 9 points. This is a BIG difference from the points that would show from just scanning the can. It isn't the WW database's fault. The can lists 1.25 cups of contents, when it really only has 1 cup in it..

Stuffing / Dressing

Tackle this turkey day hurdle with a few very smart ingredients swaps

With the holidays fast approaching, I wanted to do what I could to try and offer help, so that you CAN have a delicious and low point holiday meal, INCLUDING dressing/stuffing. You'd think that there's no way to possibly have low point dressing that doesn't taste like cardboard, but it's totally doable. You just have to be smart about it. Glance at the recipe and you'll see that all we really had to do was use low point bread. I also removed the butter. We're getting a buttery flavor by cooking with butter flavored cooking spray.

Servings Info.:

Yield: (1) 3 qt. Casserole Dish
Servings: 12
Serving Size: 3/4 cup

Points:

	G	B	P
1 serving =	2	2	2
2 servings =	5	3	3
3 servings =	7	5	5

Ingredients:

- 16 slices Sara Lee 45 Calorie Bread
  (or other brand 1 point/slice sandwich bread)
- 1 lb batch of my ground turkey Italian Sausage,
  (recipe on pg. 28, in the Foundations Section)
- Butter flavored cooking spray. (Different brands have different point values. Scan your can, make sure you use a 0 point amount for step 4.)
- 2 cups onion, diced
- 2 cups celery, diced
- 1-1/2 cups carrot, diced
- 3 cups chicken broth**
- 2 large eggs
- 2 medium garlic cloves, chopped
- 2 Tbsp fresh rosemary, finely chopped
- 2 Tbsp fresh sage, finely chopped
- 2 Tbsp fresh thyme, finely chopped
- 1 tsp onion powder
- 1 tsp garlic powder
- salt and pepper to taste

Directions:

1. Preheat oven to 250 degrees. Cut sliced bread into 1/2 inch cubes and spread onto baking sheet. Bake for 25-40 minutes, or until the bread is completely dried out, but not burned. Look in every 10 minutes after 25 minutes to check. Set aside.

2. Mix all of the ingredients for the turkey portion of the recipe in a mixing bowl until well combined. Heat a large sauce pan over medium-high heat. Spray the pan with butter flavored cooking spray and cook the meat until just cooked through. Use a kitchen utensil to break up the meat into smaller pieces during cooking. Remove from pan, set aside.

3. Dice the onions, celery, carrots, garlic and set aside. Finely chop fresh rosemary, sage and thyme.

4. Spray the pan that you cooked the ground turkey in with butter flavored cooking spray. Cook the onions, carrots, celery and garlic over medium heat for 5-6 minutes, until they begin to soften.

5. Add the chicken broth and fresh herbs to the pan, along with the garlic powder and onion powder. Cook at a low simmer for 15 minutes. Turn off the heat, stir in the turkey, season with salt and pepper. Cool for 10-15 minutes.

6. Whisk the 2 large eggs and stir them into the cooled pan of vegetables and broth. Place all of the dried bread in a large mixing bowl, pour the vegetable/broth mixture over the bread and mix to combine. Add more broth if the mixture is too dry, though it should be ok.

7. Preheat oven to 325 degrees. Pour the dressing mixture into a 3 quart (13"x9") casserole dish sprayed with butter flavored cooking spray. Gently spread the mixture out evenly. Cover the casserole dish with aluminum foil and bake for 25 minutes. After 25 minutes, take the dish out of the oven, remove the foil, and use a kitchen utensil to gently "fluff" the dressing up without breaking it apart. Return the casserole to the oven and bake uncovered for an additional 15 minutes. Done.

NOTES:

A) The store near my house only has Sara Lee 45 calorie WHOLE WHEAT bread, that's what I used. Even though it was whole wheat bread, it was still very, very tasty. There are a few different brands of sliced bread out there that are 1 point per slice. If you can't find one, then most major supermarkets (around here anyways) carry "Nature's Own" Butter Bread, which is 3 points for 2 slices. Good luck, there's low point bread out there.

B) You can stretch this even further by adding some mushrooms to the veggies, or diced apples.

C) Feel free to swap out the ground turkey for oysters or any other protein that you want. The meat gives a different texture from the mushy dressing and soft veggies, plus it stretches out an extra serving. Customize this baby.

D) Add more broth if you want your dressing to be a little mushier. It's totally your call on how you like your dressing.

E) You can also choose to bake the stuffing in individual cupcake size portions. Just scoop 3/4 cup servings into cupcake pans, cover with foil so that the dressing doesn't dry out, then bake at 325 for 20-25 minutes.

F) You can make a modified version of this dressing using my corn muffins instead of bread to make cornbread stuffing, adjust points accordingly.

G) You can let your cubed bread air dry ahead of time, rather than baking it in the oven to dry it out.

H) On the Green Plan you can substitute the 2 whole eggs with egg whites.

Sweet Potato Casserole 2.0

An awesome and low point twist on a Thanksgiving classic

In order to get this baby down in points, we need to think of how to stretch out the points from the sweet potatoes, while still keeping the integrity of the dish and a good flavor profile. To accomplish this, we've cut the sweet potato with a larger amount of 0 point items that complement it. Namely, we've created a delicious mash of roasted sweet potato, butternut squash, carrot and canned pumpkin puree. Now that's using your noodle, folks.

Servings Info.:
Yield: 9 cups
Servings: 12
Serving Size: 3/4 cup

Points:

	G	B	P
1 serving =	3	3	2
2 servings =	7	6	4
3 servings =	10	9	6

Ingredients:

- 1 pound Sweet Potato/Yam, slice in half horizontally
- 1 pound carrots, peeled (I used baby carrots for ease)
- 12 cups butternut squash, peeled and cubed. Around 4 pounds will give you 12 cups.
- 30 oz. canned pumpkin puree (0 point cans)
- 1/2 cup pecans, chopped and crushed to fit as much as you can into that 1/2 cup.
- 2 tsp ground cinnamon, divided
- 1-1/2 tsp pumpkin pie spice
- 2 tsp sugar
- 1 tsp maple extract (can be found in the spice aisle by the vanilla extract)
- 7 Tbsp sugar free maple syrup (pancake syrup)
- 2 slices turkey bacon, cooked, allowed to dry, then broken into small crumbled pieces
- 3/4 cup mini marshmallows, packed
- butter flavored cooking spray
- salt and pepper
- 2 large eggs

Directions:

1. Preheat oven to 400 degrees. Line 2 or 3 large baking sheet pans with parchment paper or foil and spray with cooking spray. Put the carrots, butternut squash and sweet potatoes into large mixing bowls (there's a lot of them). Spray to coat with butter flavored cooking spray, mix and spray to coat completely. Arrange the vegetables on the prepared sheet pans.

2. Place the veggies and squash into the oven and roast for 30 minutes at 350 degrees.

3. Remove the pans from the oven and put the carrots and butternut squash into a large container and set aside. Return the sweet potato halves to the oven and bake for an additional 15-20 minutes until soft. Remove from oven and set aside.

4. While the veggies are roasting, you'll prepare the candied pecans. Heat the pecans in a sauce pan without any butter or cooking spray on medium heat for 4-5 minutes, stirring to ensure they don't burn. When they start to get fragrant and darken in color slightly, stir in 1 tsp sugar and 1/2 tsp of cinnamon, stir to combine. Add 1 Tbsp of water and 1 Tbsp of sugar free syrup, stir until the liquid dissolves. Remove from heat and set aside in bowl.

5. Heat the pumpkin puree in a pot over medium-low heat to just warm it. Add the maple extract and all of the remaining cinnamon, pumpkin pie spice and sugar free maple syrup. Stir to mix.

6. Place the roasted squash, carrots and sweet potato into a food processor in batches and blend on high speed until processed to ALMOST a smooth puree. You want to keep some texture to it. Scoop out each batch into a large mixing bowl.

7. Add the pumpkin puree to the large mixing bowl and use a rubber spatula to fold all of the pureed vegetables and pumpkin together. Add the eggs and mix to combine.

8. Spray a large 3 quart (9"x13") casserole dish with butter flavored cooking spray, then spoon all of the mash into the dish and spread evenly.

9. Spread the mini marshmallows along the top of the sweet potato mixture, then sprinkle the toasted pecans and crushed bacon bits. Drizzle the final 2 Tbsp of sugar free syrup around the casserole.

10. Bake the casserole for 15-20 minutes at 375 degrees, or until the marshmallows are slightly brown and toasted. Remove from oven. Enjoy.

NOTES & SUGGESTIONS:

- I would ONLY recommend using the marshmallows on this if you plan to serve it within 1-1.5 hours of making it. I noticed that around 2 hours after baking that the marshmallows were starting to "deflate", and at the 3 hour mark, they were flat and in desperate need of some Viagra
- If you don't want to use marshmallows on your casserole, you can leave them off and have an extra 6 ingredient points to play with. That would allow you to add an additional 1/4 cup of candied pecans to the topping instead.
- If you would like your casserole to be a little sweeter, you can add an additional 4 teaspoons of sugar into the pumpkin puree and the total point value will still JUST barely be 3 point for the first serving, but the second serving will be 7 points. It's up to you.
- Feel free to use regular maple syrup instead of sugar free syrup, but doing so will raise the point value up to 5 points per serving.
- If you don't mind artificial sweeteners, feel free to sweeten the bajeesus out of this baby.
- RECIPE BUILDER FUN: If you input this entire recipe into the builder, on blue, it says that the first serving is 4 points. It's wrong. Scroll the servings to 0, then back to 1, and it magically changes to the correct point value of 3 points for the first serving. *eye roll*

Corn Muffins

Getting "REAL" cornbread down to 1 point. BOOMshakalaka!!!

Alright folks, I had a LOT of requests to include my cornbread muffin recipe into this Thanksgiving download because, well... cornbread. One of the first things I made when I started Weight Watchers was an old school cornbread recipe that's been floating around in-program for decades. Pretty much just cornmeal, egg, and a can of creamed corn. For the life of me, I couldn't figure out WHY they had to be 2 points each, there HAD to be a smarter way to do it. All it took was a little bit of alone time with the recipe builder, a glass of wine, some Marvin Gaye... and 9 months later we have 1 point cornbread. Seriously though... instead of the creamed corn, which has points, blend up a can of 0 point corn, with a bit of sweetener. Boom, goodbye 11 points. Then I saw that corn flour has slightly less points than cornmeal So, by using a mix of corn flour AND cornmeal we're able to drop these babies down to 1 point each for the first 2 muffins. What's the moral of the story? Get creative in the recipe builder.

Ingredients:

- 1-1/4 cups masa harina (corn flour)
- 3/4 cup yellow cornmeal
- 3 tsp baking powder
- 3 large eggs
- 3/4 tsp salt
- 3 Tbsp 0 point sweetener o' choice (monkfruit, swerve, stevia, splenda, etc)**
- (2) 15oz cans whole kernel corn with their liquid
    - Scan it to make sure you pick 0 point cans of corn (on **blue** and **purple**). Scan Scan Scan.
- 1/2 cup whole corn kernels
(in addition to the above listed corn)
- 1 Tbsp of skim milk or almond milk

Directions:

1. Preheat oven to 400 degrees.
2. Line cupcake/muffin tins with liners. I personally like to use foil liners because I am cursed. Any time that I use the paper liners, EVERYTHING always sticks to them. Yes, even with spray. I hate paper liners. I only used them in the pic up top because I was out of foil ones. Paper liners = evil.
3. Put the corn flour and yellow cornmeal into a large mixing bowl, along with the baking powder, salt and sweetener. Stir to combine.
4. Beat the 3 large eggs in a mixing bowl until they are crying and hand over their lunch money. Set aside.
5. Put the entire contents of the 2 cans of 0 point corn, as well as the sweetener and milk into a blender, food processor, or use an immersion blender. Pulse it a few times to to roughly process the corn together with the liquid and sweetener, into a rough chopped corny slurry. Congrats, you've just replaced high point canned corn with a 0 point substitute. Booooom goes the dynamite.

Servings Info.:
Yield: 24 muffins
Servings: Umm... 24. 🤪
Serving Size: 1 muffin

Points: Ⓖ Ⓑ Ⓟ

	G	B	P
1 serving =	2	1	1
2 servings =	4	2	2
3 servings =	7	4	4
4 servings =	9	5	5

6. Pour the blended corn mixture into a mixing bowl with the dry ingredients, along with 1/2 cup of whole corn kernels and the beaten eggs, which should still be crying about being mugged. Mix it all together until well combined. Set aside and let it rest for 10 minutes.
7. Fill the cupcake liners 3/4 full. The batter should have fluffed up a little bit while it was resting.
8. Bake at 400 degrees for 14-18 minutes. Mine took 16.

NOTES:

- YES, THESE ARE REGULAR SIZED! There is a special place in the lake of fire for people who give out muffin and cupcake recipes that are for MINI baked goods and don't tell you they are. Then you get your hopes all up and are all "hurray, muffins!" Then you make them and are all sad, like when you found out about the Easter Bunny.
- If you are using a shiny, thin cupcake pan, they seem to take longer to cook than if you are using a darker, thick nonstick cupcake or muffin pan.
- You can substitute the 2 Tbsp of sweetener with 2 Tbsp of regular sugar if you'd like, but adjust your points accordingly. Also, if you like sweeter cornbread, add more sweetener.
- Want to add a little bit of 0 point buttery flavor? Spray a few blasts of butter flavored cooking spray into the dough, while mixing.
- People in Connect have been making batches of these muffins and using them to make cornbread stuffing with a modified version of my stuffing recipe.
- **On the GREEN plan? Sub the eggs with 2 egg whites to keep the points in line with the BLUE & PURPLE plans.**

Spiced Cranberry Sauce

This is worlds removed from that canned goop you're used to

I tried my best to make as many low point side dishes as able this past Thanksgiving, but I naturally wasn't able to make everything that people requested. The most requested side that I couldn't get to was Cranberry Sauce. THANKFULLY, a wonderful friend from Connect, "@mugglemama2017" came to the rescue. She gave me permission to include her amazing Spiced Cranberry Sauce in this section.

Her cranberry sauce is a low point thing of beauty. It's sweet, tangy, has tremendous depth of flavor from the cinnamon, cloves, nutmeg, allspice, ginger and orange zest. Throw in a little bit of spiced rum and you won't even care about eating the main course, you'll be off, huddled in a corner with a bowl of this sauce and a spoon. You'll probably be clutching it like Gollum from The Lord of The Rings, calling it "Myyyy Preeeeecious" and snarling at passers-by.

Servings Info.:
Yield: 4 cups
Servings: 16
Serving Size: 1/4 cup

Points:

	G	B	P
1 serving =	0	0	0
2 servings =	1	1	1
3 servings =	1	1	1
4 servings =	1	1	1

Ingredients:

- 24 ounces fresh or frozen cranberries, divided
- 1-1/3 cup 0 point sweetener o' choice*** *(monkfruit, stevia, swerve, splenda, etc)*
- 2 tsp molasses***
- 3/4 cup water, divided
- 1-1/2 tsp cornstarch
- 2 tablespoons orange juice
- Zest from 1 orange
- 2 teaspoons ground cinnamon
- 1/2 teaspoon ground allspice
- 1/2 teaspoon salt
- 1/2 teaspoon freshly grated nutmeg
- 1/8 teaspoon ground ginger
- 1/8 teaspoon ground cloves *(optional)****
- 1 tablespoon spiced rum *(optional)****

NOTES:

- In this recipe, I'm using regular sweetener and molasses, in place of brown sugar. Other options could be:
  * **Real Brown Sugar:** Pretty obvious, but adjust points.
  * **0 Point Brown Sugar Substitutes:** Sukrin Gold, Swerve, Lakonta Monkfruit and Splenda, all make 0 or low point brown sugar replacements.
  * **Root Beer:** Yep, sounds funky, but it's a viable option. Root beer has a complex caramel flavor and though it WILL change the flavor profile slightly, 1/4 cup of root beer is only 1 ingredient point. Or you could replace ALL of the water with diet rootbear.
- I have the cloves as optional, because my wife HATES the taste of cloves, in anything.
- If you don't want to use spiced rum, you can either leave it out, or you can substitute it with 1 teaspoon of rum extract, which can be found in the spice aisle next to the vanilla extract.

Directions:

1. Place half (12 oz) cranberries, sweetener, molasses, 1/2 cup water, cornstarch, orange juice, orange zest, cinnamon, allspice, salt, nutmeg, ginger and cloves (if using) into a pot. Bring to a boil over medium heat.
2. Cook, stirring occasionally until most berries start to pop, about 10 minutes. Add the other 12 oz. of cranberries, the remaining 1/4 cup water, then cook for an additional 5-10 minutes or until most of the new berries have popped.
3. Remove from heat, stir in spiced rum (if using), and let cool for 30 minutes. Adjust consistency with additional water, as needed.
4. Serve immediately or place in an airtight container and store in the refrigerator. Reheat prior to serving.

Pumpkin Spice Cake

Crammed with so much pumpkin spice, it'll make your seasonal latte jealous

This is, hands down, one of my favorite cakes. It's insanely easy to make, comes together REALLY quickly and is so moist and fluffy that you won't believe it. I loved it, my wife, who can't stand pumpkin pie spice anything, still didn't like it... So that's how I knew it was juuuust right 😊. Imagine if you will, a sexy pumpkin pie, going out to a club, having a few drinks, then hooking up with a tall dark and handsome pumpkin cake. The two elope to Vegas... then 9 months later, this cake would be the logical byproduct of said-union.

Serving Info.:

YIELDS: 12 slices
Points: 1 slice = 5 points
      2 slices = 9 points
      3 slices = 14 points

Points:***

	G	B	P
1 serving =	5	5	5
2 servings =	9	9	9
3 servings =	14	14	14
4 servings =	19	18	18

In the Builder, at 1 serving, the Blue plan shows the first serving at 6 points. Scroll the servings to 0, then back to 1 and it resets to the correct value of 5 points. The recipe builder is a buggy biznitch, sometimes.

Ingredients:

Cake Batter:
- 1 sugar free yellow cake mix
- 1 (15oz) canned pumpkin puree *(Pick a 0 point can, scan it)*
- 1 egg *(optional though HIGHLY recommended for texture)*
- 1 tsp baking powder
- 2 tsp ground cinnamon
- 2 tsp pumpkin pie spice
- 1 tsp McCormick's maple extract (or other brand)
- 2 tsp McCormick's Pumpkin Pie Spice EXTRACT
- 1-1/3 cup carbonated water or diet soda (root beer)

Pumpkin Spice Puree Frosting
- 2 (15oz) cans pumpkin puree *(pick 0 point cans, scan them)*
- 1 (1oz) box sugar free Jello instant butterscotch pudding
- 1 (1oz) box sugar free Jello instant vanilla pudding
- 2 tsp pumpkin pie spice
- 1-1/2 tsp ground cinnamon
- 1-1/2 tsp McCormick's Pumpkin Pie Spice EXTRACT

Topping:
- 1/4 tsp ground cinnamon
- fine mesh, wire strainer

Directions:

1. Preheat oven to 325.
2. Line the bottom of 2 round 9" cake pans with parchment paper. Spray the sides with cooking spray, set aside.

*** CAKE DIRECTIONS
3. In a large mixing bowl, combine the cake mix, egg, pumpkin puree, baking powder, cinnamon, pumpkin pie spice, and the extracts. Pour in the carbonated liquid of choice (I used seltzer water) and mix.
4. Pour the batter into the 2 prepared 9" round cake pans. Use a measuring scoop to try and fill each pan with a relatively equal amount, so that they bake up close to the same height.
5. Bake at 325 for 30-35 minutes, or until a toothpick inserted into the center comes out clean. Cooking times may vary depending on your oven, altitude... or attitude.
6. When the toothpick comes out dry, remove the cakes from the oven and allow to cool to room temperature.

*** FROSTING DIRECTIONS
7. Using an electric mixer, mix together the 2 cans of pumpkin puree, instant pudding packets, pumpkin pie spice, cinnamon and pumpkin pie spice EXTRACT. Mix until well combined and smooth.
8. Cover and place in the refrigerator for 30 minutes to set.

*** ASSEMBLY

9   Remove one of the cake layers from the pans and place it on a serving dish or platter, flat side down.

10 Scoop all of your pumpkin puree frosting into a 1 gallon sized ziplock bag. Twist the bag, while forcing all of the frosting down to 1 corner of the bag. Use scissors to snip an index finger-width hole in the bag's corner, to make a piping bag.

11 Cover the bottom cake layer with a layer of frosting, about as tall as your pinky finger is wide. Pipe a second layer of frosting on top of the first, to create a thick layer of filling for the cake.

12 Take your second cake layer, and flip it upside down, so that the perfectly flat bottom, which was on the bottom of the cake pan, will now be the top of your cake. Gently push down on the top cake layer, to sliiiiightly press it down into the pumpkin filling.

13 Frost the top of the cake, from edge to edge, with a thin layer of the pumpkin puree. You want to try and leave enough puree to pipe more around the entire edge of the cake. So just spread a thin layer on top.

14 Put the remaining 1/4 tsp of cinnamon into a small wire strainer and dust all over the top of the cake, to lightly coat the frosting.

15 Pipe small mounds of the pumpkin puree all around the outer edge of the cake. You can use a decorative piping tip if you'd like it to look snazzier.

*** NOTES

-   If you cannot find pumpkin pie spice EXTRACT at your local grocery stores, you might be able to purchase it online at walmart.com. You can then have it delivered to a local walmart for free in-store pickup.

-   IF you have no luck, you can always just use maple extract. The final flavor will be different, but it will still be very tasty.

-   You can leave out the 1 egg from the batter if you wish, however, the cake WILL be light and fluffy, but extremely delicate. When I made it without the egg, it was light, fluffy and delicious, but it would start to break when I'd pick up the finished cake layers. Adding 1 egg helps hold it together, though it's not absolutely necessary. I care about you ultra strict vegan hipsters too. 😊

"Gringo" Tamales

REAL tamales, made with my low point & fat Masa recipe

Ok, I'm going to start off by stating the obvious. Tamale purists, do NOT read the rest of this write up yet. You need to immediately drive to UC Berkeley, go to one of their designated "safe spaces", then get ready to picket. These are not traditional tamales... but they are freaking good, low calorie, virtually fat free and can be used as a healthier blank canvas. Fill them with whatever you want, use whatever sauce you want... but adjust your points accordingly.

I am providing less of a recipe and more of a GUIDE for how to make these. I am using foil, rather than cornhusks, on purpose. 99% of the people reading this have never made Tamales and for them, the thought of going to a store to find corn husks, soak them in water then trying to use them, is a no-go. But... EVERYONE has foil. Again, use this as a GUIDE. If you want to use corn husks, USE CORN HUSKS. Use this Gringo Tamale Guide as a template.

Tamales with shredded chicken breast and roasted tomatillo sauce.
3 points for 1, 6 points for 2 on *BLUE* & *PURPLE*.

IMPORTANT:

- The points provided to the right, are for a 2 cup batch of my low point Masa (recipe pg. 38-39), sectioned into 8 separate 1/4 cup dough portions. From there, the points will vary depending on what YOU use for filling and for a sauce. In the picture above I used shredded chicken breast with my 0 point Tomatillo sauce (recipe pg. 79). In the recipe-guide pictures to the right, they were filled with my low point chorizo.

Ingredients:

- 1 (2 cup) batch of my Low Point Masa, recipe pg. 38-39
  - Make sure you add the additional baking powder and do the chicken broth swap to the Masa, as indicated in the recipe.

Filling Ideas:

- Shredded/Chopped chicken breast, pork, beef, veggies, cheese, heck... even fruit. There are sweet tamales too.

Sauce Ideas:

- My low point red enchilada sauce (pg 77), roasted tomatillo sauce (pg 79), Mexican Mole' sauce (pg 74), or even a simple fruit puree with a little chili powder or cayenne pepper added, for use with sweet fruit tamales (strawberry and pineapple are popular).

Wrappers:

- 8 decent sized squares of foil wrap, oooooooor....
- 8 packaged, store bought corn husks, soaked

Note:

Remember, I'm showing how to make these with foil wrap. It's a near-identical process using corn husks. Watch a quick youtube video on making Tamales to see how to use traditional corn husks. If you see it one time, that's all you need. My goal here is to make this as accessible to as many people as possible.

Servings Info.:

Yield: 8 Tamales
Servings: 8
Serving Size: 1 Tamale

Points: Ⓖ Ⓑ Ⓟ

	G	B	P
1 serving =	3	3	3
2 servings =	7	6	6
3 servings =	10	9	9
4 servings =	13	13	13

Directions:

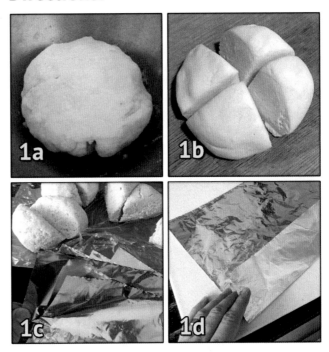

1 **(A)** Make a 2 cup batch of my Masa, as indicated in the recipe on pg 38. Cut the ball into 2 equal portions, then **(B)** cut each big masa ball into 4 equal 1/4's. **(C)** Tear off 8 sections of foil wrap, 1 for each tamale. **(D)** Lay each one down on a cutting board or counter and fold the bottom 1/4 up and onto itself. This is only done so that the foil isn't so much larger than the tamales when we roll them up.

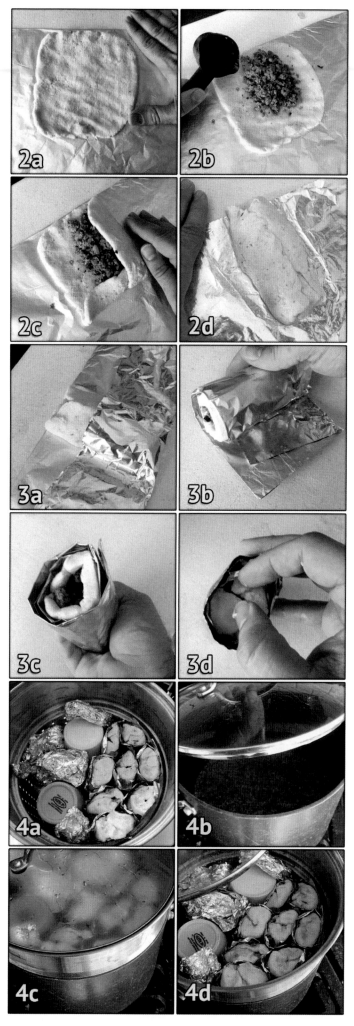

2. **(A)** Spray the foil with cooking spray, then lightly wet your hands. Press a 1/4 section of Masa down onto the foil, using your hands to create a shape similar to what's pictured. Just to the top of the foil. **(B)** Add whatever filling you will be using, leaving some exposed masa on the sides. **(C)** Fold the bottom up and onto the filling, then fold one side up, followed by the second side. **(D)** Join the two sides in the center and lightly press to join the two folds.

3. **(A)** Fold the bottom of the foil up and over the tamale. **(B)** Roll the tamale in the foil, not too loose, not too tight. Just like the 3 little bears, make it juuuuust right. **(C)** Ta da!!!! **(D)** Gently press the exposed masa together. Rinse and repeat steps 2 and 3 until all of the tamales are rolled.

4. **(A)** Place the tamales in the bottom of a large stock pot steamer insert (page 11). You want to place them in so that the seam of each foil-wrapped tamale is pressed against the wall of the metal insert, or up against another tamale. You don't want them to unravel while steaming. Fill the empty space of the insert with upside down mugs and wadded up tin foil. The mugs help take up space without wasting too much additional foil. **(B)** Fill the bottom of your stock pot with enough water to JUST stop underneath the insert, then bring the water to a boil. Do NOT have the tamales in yet. Just heat up the water. **(C)** Once your water is boiling, place the insert, with the tamales, into the steamer and cover with the lid. Reduce the flame to medium. **(D)** Steam the tamales for 25 minutes. Done.

NOTES:
- As noted, the actual points of YOUR tamales will vary based upon your filling and sauce. The points shown on page 98 are just for the (8) 1/4 cup sections of masa.
- These are great as is. You can DEFINITELY use corn husks instead of foil, but it won't really do anything other than give the outsides a prettier appearance AND it's traditional. Trust me, I would NEVER prepare them in foil for my wife's Mexican family… it would not end well for this Gringo.
- A common sweet treat that you'll find at Tamale shops are fruit infused tamales. You can add cooked down berries or crushed pineapple to the masa, to give it a colored hue and some sweetness.
- Sweet corn and green chili & cheese are two more common fillings. I've even seen recipes for "chocolate" tamales, with cocoa powder added to the masa, for color, filled with chicken and brown mole' sauce.
- You can watch a video of me making the tamales in Connect, under the hashtag #dhallaktamales. I also have the video in my Youtube channel, The Guilt Free Gourmet.

Closing Thoughts

The Writings of Lord Daniel von Hallakstein

Lord Daniel von Hallakstein VII, Ruler of Gluttonia *(1573-1622)*
Protector of Gluttons, Slayer of Points & Keeper of the Seven Spices

As you've probably realized by now, this isn't a full fledged, stand-alone cookbook. This is a quasi instructional cooking guide, that I want you to use to begin creating. I want to encourage you to use the recipes in here, along with the ideas for ingredient swaps and the recipe builder tutorial, to start playing around with recipes. Open up cookbooks, go online to food websites, look up delicious high calorie dishes, then put them in the builder and start tweakin'.

This book contains everything that you'll need to completely o-freakin-bliterate any feelings of helplessness that you've had with your meals. Is your husband a non-supportive schmo that complains about your "diet cooking?" That doesn't have to be the case anymore. Are you stressing about how much you miss one dish or another? Hack it down. Sub out the Italian sausage for my recipe, replace the the heavy cream with some almond milk and cornstarch... you can do this.

If there is one thing that I would ask of you, it's that you PLEASE share with me your triumphs and setbacks in the kitchen. We're all stronger together and we're all walking the same path. If you use my Recipe Builder tutorial to tweak a recipe to be lower in points and you want to show that baby off? Post it in Connect! Use the hashtag *#RecipeBuilderChallenge*, along with what the original points per servings were, followed by what you lowered it to with your tweaks. After playing with recipes a few times, through trial and error, you'll find techniques that really work for you. Share those in your post so they might help others. Need help with a recipe? Ask! Heck, feel free to submit a question to me directly through info@theguiltfreegourmet.net, or shoot me a message on Connect. I'll respond if I see it... and remember. If I don't, I probably missed it, so resend it, I don't mind. Guys are forgetful, it's a curse.

Though this IS a stand alone cooking guide, this book will be **ESSENTIAL** for my upcoming cookbook. Almost every single dish there will reference foundation recipes that are found in this book. In my cookbook, as an example, I can't type out the ingredient lists for all of the foundation recipes, into every Appetizer recipe that calls for them. As an example, on the chorizo stuffed tamale balls, I can't take an entire page to add the recipe for my chorizo, my low point masa & my roasted tomatillo sauce, into that recipe. I will simply make a note that the recipe calls for *"1lb batch of my chorizo, pg # of the cooking guide" "2 cups prepared Masa, pg # of the cooking guide"* etc. Consider this to be the 1st Volume of my cookbook, where the actual main dish recipes begin in volume 2 and reference foundation recipes and sauces in this book. I'd like to combine it all together into one big SUPER BOOK... but it would cost too much on Amazon.

With that said, thank you so much for your support and enouragement through this entire project. Thank you for allowing me the opportunity to be able to help you in your journey, as well as for helping me be able to feel like I'm helping make a difference. Now that we all have the warm fuzzies goin', remember,

YOU'VE GOT THIS!!!!

Acknowledgements

Well here we are again. When I wrote my acknowledgements for the first edition of this book, back in 2018, I never in a MILLION YEARS would have imagined that it would ever blow up to the point that it has. I started the entire project out of a desire to help folks, but then a crazy thing happened, ya'll ended up helping me just as much. As most of you stay at home parents know, you lose your sense of self and personal worth, when your entire purpose, day in and day out... is to just stay shut in your house, changing diapers and shuttling kids around. Suddenly, this whole book went full-on best seller. In just over 10 months, it was downloaded over 350,000 times and sold over 11,000 copies. I started getting emails from people all across the country, telling me how it had completely changed their lives and given them hope with their weight loss journeys.

I had one sweet lil grandma tell me how she made tamales for the first time in her life, for her picky husband who always picked on her "diet cooking", how much he loved them and how wonderful she felt. A mom sending me a video of her and her young daughter making fresh pasta together for the first time, complete with the adorable little girl narrating "look Daniel, we're doing it!" Pictures of a family sitting around their Christmas dinner table, full of my holiday dishes, all smiling for the camera. A woman who made one of my sugar free cakes for her diabetic father... and on, and on, and on... I cannot even begin to express to you folks how much you have all touched my life and changed me as a person, because of all of this.

I started all of this because all of you, in Connect, badgering me to do it in the Spring of 2017. When I had to resign from my job, to stay home and take care of Jesse and Rachel, I never would have thought that my website and graphics experience would ever be used for anything, ever again, other than maybe getting a tiny side job every now and then... and look where we are now. Folks, this was the perfect storm. There are people in Connect who could haaaaaaands down cook me under the table any day of the week and twice on Sunday. Mappleby777, Longhorn_Sooner, and Hannahamil, just to name a few. There are some fanTASTIC cooks in Connect that you all should definitely be following. I just got lucky because I have experience doing graphics layouts, otherwise we wouldn't be here.

Well, with that lil bit of instrospection out of the way, I'll try to rattle off a few names of people who were very important to this Second Edition getting made. In the first book I named nearly 40-50 people. I can't do that this time, I'd leave too many people out, on accident. I'm following over 3,000 people so I can't mention all of you, but know that I ONLY click to follow you if you've said or done something that has connected with me personally. So even if you're not mentioned in here, I still thank you.

As always, @*Andmatsmom*. Honestly, Lady, I'll convert you to sweeteners someday. Come to the dark side! 😈 *MariaRachael* and *Missvw40*, my 2 sisters from other misters. *Kygoatgirl* and all of my Elizabethtown homies... I'll get out there, I promise! 69gabybal, the poor lady that I'm probably slowly turning into an alcoholic, as I force her to try and fix all of my typos and grammar. Cake.Riot, for providing all of the nutritional information for my recipes.

Thank you, of course, to my wife, who continues to put up with me. My kids, for turning me into a better person, despite all of the stains on my clothes now. And lastly, I'll thank my Mom, who made me first start thinking about the need to modify recipes specifically for people with dietary restrictions. You'll never know what an impact it had on me, that one Thanksgiving... seeing you standing there eating a hamburger patty out of a ziploc bag, from your purse, while all of us were piling our plates high with food... and you couldn't eat any of it because of your heart... and none of us had taken that into consideration. There was nothing you could eat, at Thanksgiving. I'll never get that image out of my mind. I just wish you could have been here long enough for me to cook for you, now that I'm actually good at it. Plus... I'm pretty sure that you would have loved Jesse and Rachel.

Book Index

A Roadmap For The Madness

Daniel Bonaparte - Emperor of France 1769-1821

Might I recommend the Bechamel sauce? Viva la France!

Made in the USA
Columbia, SC
12 December 2019